JAMIL
CHILD OF LIGHT

Messenger of God

By Gene Savoy Sr

THE SACRED TEACHINGS OF LIGHT
CODEX 1

JAMIL
CHILD OF LIGHT

Messenger of God

By Gene Savoy Sr

JAMILIAN UNIVERSITY PRESS

Jamil: Child Of Light,
Messenger Of God The Sacred Teachings Of Light - Codex 1

COPYRIGHT © 1973, 1976, 1995, 2008, 2022

Full Use Of This Volume Is Subject To Oral Instruction As Administered In The Jamilian University Of The Ordained Of The International Community Of Christ, Church Of The Second Advent, By Its Authorized And Licensed Teachers, Ordained And Under Pastorship Papers.

No Part Of This Publication May Be Reproduced, Stored In A Retrieval System, Or Transmitted In Any Form Or By Any Means, Electronic, Mechanical, Photocopying, Recording, Or Otherwise Without Prior Written Permission From The Publishers.

Trademarks: The Second Advent Cross And Seal; "International Community Of Christ"; "Church Of The Second Advent"; "Jamilian"; And "Cosolargy" Are Registered Trademarks Of The International Community Of Christ.

Copyright © 2008 International Community Of Christ, A Corporation Sole. Copyright © 1973 Gene Savoy. Copyright © Under The Universal Copyright And Berne Conventions. All Rights Reserved.

Copyright fuels creativity, encourages diverse voices, promotes free speech, and creates a vibrant culture. Thank you for buying an authorized edition of this book and for complying with copyright laws by not reproducing, scanning, or distributing any part of it in any form without permission.

Published In The United States Of America By The International Community Of Christ, 643 Ralston Street, Reno, Nevada, 89503. Printed By The Jamilian University Press.

EBOOK ISBN 978-1-949360-07-3
PRINT EDITION ISBN 978-1-949360-12-7

Library Of Congress Catalogue Number: 73-92360

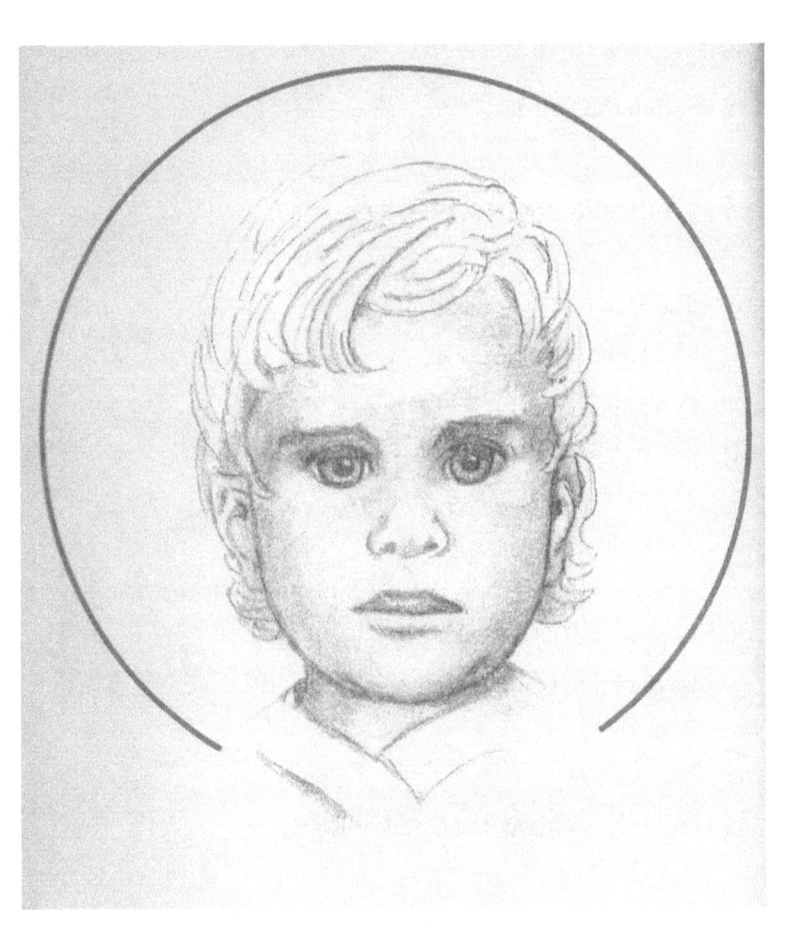

CONTENTS

Preface

Note from the Editors

TEXT I | THE BEGINNING: 1955-59

1. The Man
2. The First Omen
3. A Light
4. The Third Omen
5. The Revelation
6. The Calling Out
7. Angels of Light Appear in the Sun
8. Laying on of Hands
9. Birth of The Child Announced
10. Rebirth
11. The Woman
12. Holy Ones Guard The Child of Light

TEXT II | LIFE WITH THE CHILD: 1959-62

13. Birth of The Child of Light
14. Oppression
15. Yungay
16. Beatification
17. Homage from a Wanderer
18. Transfiguration
19. The Living Communion Exemplified
20. The Final Meal
21. The Mountain Falls
22. The Comforter
23. The Prophecy
24. The Divine Command

TEXT III | THE REVELATION: 1962

25. The Child Returns to the Worlds of Light
26. At the Sepulcher
27. The Sun of Righteousness Proclaimed

PREFACE

THIS BOOK IS A BRIEF documented and historical account of the acts and revelations of a Miraculous Seer Child who left a spiritual legacy that continues to astound and inspire seekers of truth the world over.

The legacy has been preserved to assure that those few evolved souls for whom it was intended may fall heir to the transforming Teachings revealed. The present text and the following series of fourteen bound volumes that treat of the Prophecies and Sayings revealed by the gifted infant are supplemented by Oral Teachings not put to the printed word. In- deed, without the Oral Teachings, the written texts cannot be fully understood, which follows in the tradition of the early Messianic Church whose mystics transmitted concealed teachings to their disciples by word of mouth—a practice which was the standard of instruction in the early closed Church that preceded the later open, public Church with its New Testament scriptures.

That the secret Oral Teachings have been lost to the Churches is generally recognized by scholars. Now restored, the Oral Teachings constitute a regenerating process which not only gives new meaning to the mystery of Christ's message, but extends to the sincere seeker the authentic methods employed by early Christians for rebirth of the spiritual Light Body. It is noteworthy that the process has been restored, amended and supplemented with vital, new techniques for use by moderns existing under entirely new environmental conditions. Once experienced by knowledgeable and competent mystics adept at applying it, the transforming process testifies to the power and truth of universal cosmic laws.

Those with a background in the Judaeo-Christian tradition may discover for themselves that the Child's Teachings, Sayings and Prophecies give greater meaning to their religious beliefs rather than detract from them.

That an authoritative Seer Child should appear in modern times is not without prophetic precedent. The final descent of a cosmic being in the guise of a Child Genius, a bringer of peace and truth, has a long history behind it, spanning many thousands of years. Fragments of recovered Dead Sea Scrolls left by the monks of Qumran, or the Essenes, from which Jesus is believed to have sprung, mention an expected Wondrous Child, a Divine Counsellor, bearing unmistakable body marks, who would come at a future time to inaugurate a new age. Chosen of God, his life and very breath were to be pre-ordained. Like Moses and Jesus, who displayed advanced full-grown natures early in life, the Child Prodigy would attain early maturity in his second year, revealing heavenly knowledge to which the average mortal does not have access. In addition, the heaven-sent Child would serve as a precursor of some great future cosmic event (from fragmentary scroll texts from the Qumran Dead Sea Literature).

> In the Hebrew scriptures, the Prophet Isaiah wrote of a coming new age of peace at a time when "The wolf shall live with the lamb, the leopard shall lie down with the kid, the calf and the young lion and the fatling together, and a little child shall lead them." (Isaiah 11:6)

Jesus, who often spoke in cryptic parables to his disciples, mentions the coming Child in allegorical terms: "At that time the disciples came to Jesus and asked, 'Who is the greatest in the Kingdom of Heaven?' He called a child, whom he put among them, and said, 'Truly I tell you, unless you change and become like children, you will never enter the Kingdom of Heaven. Whoever becomes humble like this child is the greatest in the Kingdom of Heaven. Whoever welcomes one such child in my name welcomes me.'" (Matthew 18:1-5)

The mystical Gospel of Thomas contains secret words spoken by Jesus to Thomas, which again refer to the "little child." Jesus says: "Let the old man heavy with days hesitate not to ask the little child of seven days about the place of life, and he will live." At another time, Thomas asks Jesus just prior to his crucifixion: "Lord, why does the visible light which shines for men's sake, rise and set?" The Savior says, "O blessed Thomas, the visible light shines for your sakes, that you might not remain in this place, but that you might come out of it. But when all the elect lay aside the animal nature, then the light will withdraw to its true being, and its true being will take it to itself." Later on Jesus says: "If they say to you,

'From where have you originated?' Say to them, 'We have come from the light, where the light has originated through itself, and it revealed itself in their image.' If they say to you, 'Who are you?' Say, 'We are his sons and we are the elect of the living Father.'"

These words reflect Jesus' claim that he came from an other world, a world of Light, or the Kingdom of Heaven.

Ancient Persian books speak of a coming Child who will be taken out of the world but who will manifest himself in Light. He is called the "Child of the Word." It is said that after his passing, great prodigies would appear in the sky, and a Light would be seen shining, a Light that would outshine that of the sun.

There exists in India an ancient mythic tradition that at some future time a Miraculous Babe, the Mahapurusa Cakravartin, would come into the world. This legend goes back to the earliest Vedic tomes, the oldest sacred writings of Hinduism, and before, to the pre-Aryan traditions of India. Mention is made of this legendary Babe in various Buddhist and Jaina writings and in the Hindu Puranas, as well as in many other works. The best description of the Cakravartin is to be found in the Buddhist Pali Canon of Ceylon. The Miraculous Babe would be recognized by distinguishing marks on his body. His coming into the world would be to fulfill man's longing for universal peace and tranquility under a just and creative cosmic power.

The Wonder Child would be accompanied by a luminous sun set in the firmament; indeed, the symbol of the Cakravartin is the neolithic sun-wheel, in essence, the sun. He would proclaim that the old sun, the light and life of the world, would experience a transformation. The new sun would shine healing rays upon all living things without distinction.

An Islamic legend tells of a coming "Divinely Guided One," the Mahdi, the awaited deliverer. With the advent of the Mahdi, mankind would experience, or enjoy, greater blessings than ever before. The term "Man of the Mahd" (cradle) is given reference. Another story recites that the Mahdi shall live five or seven or nine years only, and then be taken out of the world. The Mahdi, it was said, would be marked with the Seal of Prophecy.

In ancient Egypt, the principal religion was that of the Light, the Father of Illumination. It is interesting to note that in the center of the Temple of Annu was the Hall of the Altar with entrances facing east towards the rising sun and west towards the setting sun. Beyond this hall was the great Hall of the Child, depicted in his cradle. There were also other representations of the Sun Child sitting in a lotus.

The future advent of the Miraculous Babe, the boy child endowed with fabulous attributes and marked with auspicious body signs, was also recorded in the Zoroastrian Zend-Avesta as well as in the ancient and revered Sibylline Oracles of apocalyptic imagery honored by Jews and later by Christians. The Oracles inspired Virgil's epic fourth Eclogue, the most discussed poem in Latin literature, that treats of the Wonder Child of God to be sent as a king from the sun, at whose birth the transformation of nature and the intensification of the Golden Age-signs would begin.

> "But at the time when heavenly grace shall rule, and when a holy child one day shall utterly destroy all wickedness, opening for baleful mortals the abyss." (Eclogue IV)

> "Thrice happy who shall live unto that time, man or woman… For good law shall come in its fullness from the starry heaven upon men, and good justice…" (Sib. Orac. 3.371-374)

> "And then from the sunrise God shall send a king, who shall give every land relief from the bane of war." (Sib. Orac. 3.652-653)

The transformation of nature and the intensification of the sun are to be the first apocalyptic signs of the dawning of a Golden Age. Malachi, God's messenger, prophesied this event with the words: "But for you who revere my name the Sun of Righteousness shall rise with healing in its wings. You shall go out leaping likes calves of the stall. (Malachi 4:2)

The Mandeans, who were said to have descended from the remaining Jewish tribes in Babylonia and who traced their ancestry to John the Baptist, preserved ancient scripture that has much in common with the Essene literature recently uncovered in the Dead Sea area at Qumran. Their religion speaks of the Powers of Light and Darkness and of the two spirits of man. The following eschatological quotations from the Ginza, or Great Book, refer to the "Messenger of Light" who appears over the ages to open the way of salvation for mankind:

"I am the Messenger of Light

whom the great God sent into the world.

The true Messenger am I,

in whom there is no falsehood.

Whoever receives God's word and doctrine his eyes are filled with light and his mouth is filled with praise and his heart is filled with wisdom... I prepared a way for the good ones and made a gateway for the world."

The present text records the short but wondrous life of The Child Jamil✠ who appeared in our modern age. He was a Messenger of Light whose revelations give new hope for mankind's spiritual aspirations. As a supernatural Messenger, he was aloof to the admiration and praise of others, but he endowed the world with the keys to salvation. That he passed away at the age of three years seems to be in keeping with the following Mandaic prophecy that tells of the Messenger of Light abandoning mankind and returning to the immortal realms:

"How many times have I come into the world? How many times they took not notice of me. With my final proclamation I depart the world never to return.

My spirit and soul return to God."

The story depicted in this book is true. The principals were real, living persons who have not been named to protect their privacy. The man described in these pages was an international figure of some renown who has since passed from this world. Although the religious work to which he dedicated his life is not generally known to the public, he did share the treasured Teachings which were entrusted into his care with those who vowed to keep them inviolate.

NOTE FROM THE EDITORS

The original text of the commentaries from 1973 has not been edited for inclusion, grammatical convention, or general readability. The words of the commentators remain as they were written by them at that time. However, wherever possible, the biographical notes on the commentators have been revised to bring them up to date. The images of Jamil, photographs of the commentators, and the group photo that appear in this volume did not appear in the original publication; they have been added for the record and to enhance the beauty of the volume.

The book JAMIL: CHILD OF LIGHT – MESSENGER OF GOD originally appeared in 1973 under the title JAMIL: THE CHILD CHRIST, and that is how the book is referenced by the commentators in this volume, whose comments were recorded in that year.

Contemporary readers may balk at the commentators' use of the terms *man* and *mankind*, and so it may be useful to explain the use of these terms.

In the effort to render the English language gender-neutral in recent years, the words "human" and "humankind" are commonly and unthinkingly used to replace the words "man" and "mankind" because the word "man" in modern times is often used in a restricted sense to refer exclusively to males.

However, this narrowing of the meaning of man reflects a constriction of overall human thought. The word *man* – like Russian *chelovek* and German *Mensch* even today – originally designated all humanity, both men and women, *as thinking, intelligent beings.*

The Latin word *humanus*, from which we get our modern human, came into Latin completely separate from humus, meaning the organic constituent of soil, but the two terms are related. Along with the term *homo*, used in the designation of our species *Homo sapiens*, these words come from a form of the Proto-Indo-European word **(dh)ghomon-*, whose literal meaning is close to "earthling" or "being of the earth," earth here referring directly to dirt or soil. This association of humankind as a "being of earth" is widespread. Even the biblical story of the origins of humankind has life being breathed into a pile of dust. It is no coincidence that the first human is named Adam, from the Hebrew *adamah*, meaning ground.

As you will learn in this book, ancient prophets and philosophers taught that *Man* was made in the Image of God, not as a physical being, for the physical body was related to the lesser nature of man, but as a Light body made in the image of the greater Light of God. This Light body was the archetype of Man – the true nature – from which evolved the physical form through some fault or transgression against God.

So while some readers might take exception to the use of the word man on the grounds that, at least in today's usage, it seems to exclude half the total number of sentient, thinking beings on the planet, we have decided to continue to use the original meaning of the English word, whose usage has been constricted and corrupted over the past ten centuries.

Hence in all our publications we continue to use the term *Man* with a capital *M*, not only in an effort to retain the association of the term with a divine as opposed to a material, earthly origin, but also to draw upon the original, uncorrupted meaning of the word man as a manifestation of "eternal Mind." For this reason, whenever you see *Man* with a capital *M*, know that this includes you.

TEXT I

THE BEGINNING

1955 - 59

1 · THE MAN

ONCE THERE LIVED in an American city a man not unlike other men, a Gentile, whose ancestors had come to the New World generations ago and willed him religious freedom. In his youth he learned the Christian ethic, and within his breast beat a desire to know and serve God✠. His was the simple faith of innocence—yet no faith was greater.

The Man was a visionary. 2

Long were the hours he spent with Scripture. Stirred by the stories of the Hebrew Prophets✠ who had prepared the Way of the Lord,✠ he longed to go back in time to the days when Jesus✠ walked the earth. He looked forward to the coming of the Savior✠ to deliver him from the bondage of matter, believing, as many others, that it was destined to occur. 3

He prayed for enlightenment and rose before dawn to sing praises to God✠ with fellow Christians. And, as manhood approached, there seemed to be no doubt of what he must do.

With rejoicing heart he bade farewell to his family and friends, intent on entering the religious life. 4

2 · THE FIRST OMEN

WHILE AT UNIVERSITY, The Man shied away from companionship and intensely sought to commune with God✠ alone in the woodlands or in the stillness of his quarters. He lived the Christian life inwardly, as mystics do. 1

One morning, while at prayer, he heard a Voice✠ speak to his Eternal Spirit✠: "The message of Christ✠ is not being transmitted by the visible Church." 2

The Voice✠ troubled him; since childhood he had been taught that a Christian must never question the authority of the Church. An inner conflict arose. His deep faith in his religion made him doubt the authenticity of The Voice✠. Again it spoke: "Return to the world and there await the message of Christ✠." 3

While he did not tell his superiors about the occurrence, he expounded on the possibility of a hidden meaning to Christ's✠ Ministry. Long-robed priests and scholars shook their heads and admonished him against heresy and blasphemy. 4

In spite of the well-intended warnings, The Man felt compelled to give up his formal studies. So it was; in June, 1948, he returned to the world, awaiting the promised event. 5

3 · A LIGHT

NOT KNOWING what God✠ intended of him, The Man devoted his energies to examining Scripture, fulfilling his Christian obligations, and earning his sustenance as did other men. 1

Time passed and he married. He continued to work by day to support his family; the nights were devoted to contemplation and scriptural readings. Still The Voice✠ did not speak. The Man found himself involved in the material world and he questioned the wisdom of having given up his religious vocation, though his family gave him much joy. 2

With the years, thousands of volumes passed under his eyes. He hoped to discover some greater meaning to Scripture that would lead him to an inner illumination. Then, on the night of August 14, 1955, seven years after the First Omen✠, he saw a great star flaming across the sky like a living torch. And again he heard The Voice✠ speaking to the ear of his God-given Soul✠. And The Voice✠ declared that those who inspired the writings of Scripture were messengers of God✠, but that the message mustneeds be learned afresh under new authority. And this was the Second Omen✠. 3

The Light✠ faded and he was alone again, inflamed with an all-consuming desire to purify himself and learn the truth. 4

4 · THE THIRD OMEN

THE MAN FELL to a deeper study of Scripture, fasting and praying for enlightenment. But, the inner meaning of Holy Writ eluded him. 1

Slowly he began to realize that the Word of God✠ is not shaped into letters and forms, imprisoned on paper, but, instead, is a living force which every man or woman must experience for himself or herself. With a humble heart he prayed for wisdom and divine guidance. 2

He sought to understand the essence of religion, to go beyond the dogma and theology of the written word. He had read the great religious works of man and discovered that many Prophets,✠ like Akhenaten✠, Moses✠, Buddha✠, Krishna✠, Lao Tzu✠, Zoroaster✠, Mohammed✠, Viracocha✠ of the Americas, and many others, had brought special messages of God✠ to their respective peoples and all shared much in common. 3

What he was seeking, he knew, must come from God✠, not through the faculties of cognition or emotion of his own being, but from an actualized Spiritual Consciousness✠ apart from his physical mind-body. 4

While Holy Men✠ of all ages taught many of the same teachings brought by Jesus✠, and shared his fate, he believed that Jesus✠—and perhaps others, too—had transmitted something special that was never put to the written word. Whatever it was, he was certain a scholarly examination would not suffice. 5

The Man put aside his books and gave his very life completely to the Spirit of Christ✠. 6

During the night of January 21, 1956, five months following the Second Omen✠, a Third Omen✠ manifested. The Man awoke from a sound sleep to discover the room flooded with a brilliant white Light.✠ Sitting upright in the bed, he stared at the center of the brilliance; though brighter than the noon-day sun, it did not hurt his eyes. It was not an earthly light, rather a luminosity from some heavenly realm. 7

As his eyes became accustomed to the radiance, he distinguished four illuminated faces forming as a vision with features so smooth and flawless they might have been formed of polished gold. They gazed upon him with iridescent eyes that shone like diamonds. Their attitude was serene and compassionate, and, though they seemed to be smiling, The Man never saw their lips move; nor did they speak. 8

Looking upon the holy scene, he stretched forth his hands and cried out: "Father✠, " in recognition of the Angels✠ of the Lord✠. 9

While The Man beheld The Light,✠ transfixed by its breathtaking grandeur, a fifth angelic figure moved forward and stationed itself directly in front of him. The glory of the Being of Light✠ shone around, and its eyes blazed like the sun. 10

As he gazed into the Light-invested Countenance✠, The Man was aware that the angelic form was communicating with him through beams of Light✠ shooting out from its eyes. In that moment he transcended the limitations of his material body. His physical mind-body was being nourished by the central Light,✠ and he lost all need of breathing. Time ceased. 11

Overcome by the celestial presence and the pervading Light✠ that covered him like a mantle, shutting out all else, The Man was joined with the Godhead✠ through a Spiritual Consciousness. And he knew he was partaking of a Holy Communion✠. 12

5 · THE REVELATION

THE VOICE of The Angel✠ spoke from within his being saying: "The New Advent✠ is approaching. One will come into the world to teach the spirits of men and to inaugurate a Christ Age✠. From earliest times it has been written that God✠ shall send a Holy One✠ at a time when the sovereignty of the world will have passed over to Christ✠ and the consummation of time will have occurred. A Religion of Light,✠ animated and inspired by the powers that brought man into being, shall manifest through the Sun of Righteousness✠ and will give birth to luminous creatures longing for unity with God✠. 1

"The Eternal Child of Light,✠ seeking to restore the world, will put on terrestrial garments and appear as other men; he shall give sight to the spiritually blind. And on this day of days, the treasure of Manna✠ will descend from on high, and the days of the Visitation✠ will have begun. That which was dead shall live again. The Seals✠ shall be opened." Having said these things, The Angel✠ fell silent. 2

The Light✠ faded. He watched the celestial figures return whence they came, noting the peaceful eyes of the nearest figure—a vision that would remain with him forever—fading away. 3

Slowly, the sensations returned to his body. He was conscious of breathing again. 4

All this time his wife lay asleep beside him, unaware of the events that had transpired. 5

The Man could not understand the significance of the vision; for, being in and of the world, he was not as yet under inspiration. But the vision gave him great peace—he drifted off to sleep, his spirit rejoicing.

He dreamt of journeying to a foreign land and of strange people; wind-swept deserts and snow-capped mountains rose up in his dreams. He found himself in vast green jungles cut by rushing rivers, among great temples of white stone perched atop lonely peaks, broken pyramids, and far-flung cities long-since abandoned by a forgotten people. 6

6 · THE CALLING OUT

THE NEXT MORNING, The Man told his wife the events of the preceding night and how they must prepare themselves for a dedicated life. She listened to his story, but alarm spread over her face when he told of the Vision of Angels✠. 1

Days later he was visited by a parish priest who questioned him about the episode; The Man told his story. The priest listened patiently, suggesting afterwards that he had experienced hallucinations. 2

The Man was at a loss to understand how a representative of a Church, dedicated to spiritual instruction, could reject visions and manifestations of the spirit. He realized his mistake of telling the story when sometime afterwards his wife abandoned him, taking their two sons. Complete ruin followed; he was stripped of material wealth, social position, home, and family. 3

The Man found himself alone in the world; he wept, cursing the injustices of man's law. But the spirit is strong, and it is often by suffering and separation from loved ones that God✠ molds and shapes men for some holy purpose. When the pain of loss passed, The Man turned to greater spiritual understanding. 4

7 · ANGELS OF LIGHT APPEAR IN THE SUN

ONE MORNING, The Man climbed a hill to collect his thoughts and plan how best to serve God✠. He often went to the forested crest, to a cave that harbored an image of the Virgin Mary. Reverently, he lit a candle and arranged a bouquet of flowers at the foot of the statue. Kneeling, he took his rosary and prayed. He remained on his knees a long time. He might have remained longer had he not felt the warmth of the rising sun falling on his shoulders and heard the song birds saluting the golden orb. He then turned from the statue and walked over to a ledge, and stood looking down upon the sleeping city, blinking in the bright light. He closed his eyes and listened to the sounds of wildlife rustling in the first light of dawn. 1

A soft breeze began to blow across his face, and the tree branches above his head danced about. The gilded rays fell on his eyelids, and he had an urge to look into the golden disk. As he slowly opened his eyes, he saw the whole horizon aglow with light. Below, the woods and grasslands, wet with mist, glistened like a carpet woven from millions of sparkling diamonds. Out of the corner of his left eye he caught sight of the delicate webbing of a spider holding dew drops, reflecting a rainbow of colors as if made of prisms. 2

He looked directly into the sun. A kaleidoscope of colors and geometric patterns swam before his vision. Like miniature suns, his eyes were linked to the greater Light;✠ they became part of a galaxy of stars, revolving around the center of the universe now throbbing as a heavenly heart. 3

As the Eternal Light✠ overflowed his being, a warmth and strength filled him, and he was at oneness with God✠. The sun transmitted all the wondrous sounds of the universe at work—a concert of glittering notes that told the story of creation. He was transcended. His eyes had touched his soul with the sun; and, as if his spirit had been imprisoned in the depths of the earth now it rejoiced, free to raise its wings towards the everlasting Light✠ whence it had come. And the Holy Spirit✠, so long at rest within, was revived. 4

And across the sun, The Man beheld the faces of the four Angels of Light✠ that had appeared to him a year earlier. They spoke as before: "Journey to Peru. There the message of Christ✠ will be revealed." Then they left him alone under the light of the eastern sky. Thereafter, it became a ritual for The Man to cast his eyes upon the sun daily at sunrise. 5

8 · LAYING ON OF HANDS

THE MAN JOURNEYED to the lands of Peru, arriving on the 14th day of April, 1957. There he was received by a group of Christian mystics who had word of his coming. Among them was a woman of middle age, a nurse by profession, with her three children: two sons and a younger daughter. After hearing the story told by The Man, she pledged to follow him. And her eldest son, a youth of but sixteen, listened to the words of the visitor. Handsome, slight of build with thin face and gaunt features, The Youth was rebellious by nature and thirsted for knowledge. He, too, agreed to follow. 1

And so it was that The Man gathered his first Companions. 2

The Man and his followers traveled to the deserts of the north. By day they walked the arid sands under a burning sun, visiting the ruined cities of ancient peoples. And The Man sat under the stars at night, contemplating the wonders of creation, awaiting a sign. Weeks and months passed, and no revelation came. But on the eve of the 21st of October of that same year, The Man experienced a Visitation✠. 3

The innumerable days under the hot, tropical sun, a strict diet of fruits and vegetables, fasting, and long hours in prayer had produced a transition. Overcome with fever, he withdrew to the cool regions of Lima, taking The Youth with him. For days he remained in his room, his body ravaged by a high temperature as though it were made of fire. 4

The Man was blessed with eyes that longed for Light✠. For weeks and months he had been eager to reunite himself with the Godhead✠. He had fused his being with The Light,✠ fixing his eyes on the bright sun from sunrise to sunset, taking his gaze from the fiery orb only when it sank below the horizon. And now his whole person was aflame with energy, radiant and brilliant to behold. He felt himself making a transition to another world where all was Light.✠ 5

As the fever mounted, he moved away from the material world; he longed to leave this mortal life. The noises from the streets, of which he had been dimly aware, were replaced by heavenly sounds—a music so beautiful, it might have come from the lips of Angels. 6

If he had to suffer death to experience what God✠ had designed for him, he was ready. It was only through this transition that he understood the answers to questions he had asked since childhood. He closed his eyes and let go, entrusting his spirit unto God✠. Freed from a great burden, his heart stopped and all was still. Then The Man became conscious of a radiant Light✠ manifesting before him which soon took the form of an Angel of God✠—a huge figure emitting Light.✠ The cosmic figure looked down on the prone mortal, extending its hands to touch his senses. 7

The Man was aware of his own stilled physical body lying in bed, yet hidden hands rose out of his spirit towards celestial realms. He gazed into the eyes of the Being of Light✠ and felt at oneness with it. It was an intimate contact between a mortal and an immortal being: spirit mingled with spirit. 8

With the touching of hands, The Man was conscious of a flow of spiritual energy coursing through his own being—an energy that gave him new vitality. And the Angel of the Lord✠ spoke: "The Gift of God✠ is everlasting Life✠. Think not that mortals gain immortality with the natural body bestowed through earthly parents, but with a greater supernatural body conceived by their Heavenly Father✠. Through Christ✠, mortals are risen from the dead, the ills of the body healed, and the spiritually blind made to see—as you have been risen, healed, and made to see, though your earthly senses are stilled. You are experiencing the Life✠ few men are given, but to which all men are heir." 9

9 · BIRTH OF THE CHILD ANNOUNCED

THE ANGEL✠ CONTINUED speaking to The Man's Eternal Consciousness✠, all the while holding his spiritual hands. "An illuminated one, self-generated, and pre-existent, is destined to come into the world as the revealer of a new teaching to fulfill the old. God✠ shall send him clothed as an innocent child, and from him will come a pure Teaching; and all the Prophets✠ of all times will honor and acknowledge him as the Light✠ of the world, for he shall be a king from The Sun.✠ 1

"You will meet a woman of the world and, taking her as your wife, unite with her. And she shall receive your seed—which shall be blessed with the spark of life—and conceive a male child, the last she will bear. The Child✠ will walk among mortals for less than four years from the moment of his conception. Prophecies will come forth for 42 months. And during those twelve hundred and sixty days a great prophecy will be given to the Churches of the world, representing the whole family of nations, and the Seven Great Seals✠ will be broken, and the Sacred Book of God✠ revealed to the world of man. 2

"His sign will be the Cross of Enlightenment and the New Sun of Righteousness✠ that will appear in great glory to alleviate the sufferings of mankind. He shall be accompanied by a multitude of Great Ones. The Child✠ will usher in a New Age for mankind. You have been chosen to be his earthly guardian—take care lest the forces of evil seek to do him harm before his time. 3

"Whilst you will be his earthly guardian and sustainer, whose energies will nourish his frail body of matter, remember that his true parents are not of this earth, for he comes from the Father✠. Therefore, let no member of the human race glorify his natural mother or father, for all members of the human family share in the motherhood and fatherhood of the Son of Man✠. Each assumes a responsibility from the moment of his coming, for the Powers of Darkness shall strive to dethrone him. 4

"The Child✠ comes not to be worshiped, but to reveal the Truth and announce to all men the means of attaining their spiritual heritage. Watch and observe his Living Communion✠ with God✠ and the Eternal Worlds of Light.✠ Bring him up in secret until the appointed time. Observe well, my son, for The Child Christ✠ and the Teachers of the world have appeared many times to many peoples of all ages, and now he appears in the Americas, his final coming and the beginning of a New World." Having said these words, The Angel✠ drew away saying: "Now return to the world. You have been raised from the dead; your life is renewed." 5

10 · REBIRTH

THEREUPON, The Man's heart began to flutter, and he drew a great breath: he lived. His mind was filled with gladness, and his spirit rejoiced. He rose from his bed and looked in a mirror. Struck by his appearance, he stood transfixed examining the reflected image—a new person. The color of his eyes had changed, and they radiated a Light.✠ Rebirth had been bestowed upon him. He knew that immortality was a joyous gift granted by God✠. It was not a matter of worship or sacrifice, not even a matter of ethics or intellectual striving. 1

Midnight approached. Being the time of the October Fair in the City of Kings, The Man was attracted by the boisterous noise of the procession gathered to pay homage to the Lord of Miracles✠. He drew near the window and looked out. Below, tens of thousands of marchers, mingled into a huge mass of worshipers, filled the night air with tormented cries and moans. They carried lighted candles and, rocking to and fro, gave the appearance of a great flame winding its way through the darkness. In the center of the mass, purple-clad bearers bore a heavily-ornamented litter upon which rested a replica of Jesus✠ crucified. Sobbing mourners pressed against them, and the bearers strained under the weight, giving the impression of a procession marching into a void, fearful and repentant. 2

The Man remained there a long time, withdrawn from the sight below, thinking that the whole meaning of Jesus✠' Christianity had escaped these poor souls. He knew that the sooner men put away the memories of Jesus'✠ earthly suffering and began to imitate his spiritual joy, the sooner they would participate in The Light.✠ He turned away, overcome by a vivid recollection of the vision so full of promise that had permitted him to understand that the True God☩ of the universe asks nothing in return, except the expression of man's own spiritual rebirth through freedom and liberation from the dark powers of ignorance. 3

He went back to bed thinking how best to communicate this message to the world. The Man realized this task surpassed his own powers, and he awaited the Promised One☩ who would speak with the power of Angels. 4

He fell asleep. 5

11 · THE WOMAN

TRUJILLO WAS THE CITY of her birth, and she grew up in the shadow of the Pyramids of the Sun and the Moon near the coast. She had inherited the grief of her family and the sorrow of her ancestors who had fallen to the mighty Inca and later to the Spaniards. As a child, she longed to be loved by an unloving father who was rich in material wealth and ruled his home with an iron hand. She was kissed by a mother whose heart was empty and embittered by the loss of a favorite son, and who stained the frocks of her children with tears. And she grew to womanhood. 1

The Woman, married and divorced, was alone with one child. 2

And it came to pass that The Man met The Woman. He spoke to her of God✠, in whom she no longer believed, and walked with her on the sandy beaches until the sun turned flaming red and sank into the azure blue sea. They sat at the pyramids watching the ancient ruins glow in the moonlight, and they listened to the soft wind blowing across the desert like whispering spirits of the dead beckoning the living. When everything became still and the stars wheeled overhead, The Man spoke of a coming Child✠ and the dedicated life that could be hers. 3

And in God's✠ good time they were united as one. 4

Each saw The Sun✠ glowing in the other's eyes, and the energies of the universe surged through their bodies. They took part in a sacred act in which their physical bodies became consecrated to the creative force. A higher power took hold of them, and their souls touched God✠. In that moment, two iridescent figures materialized before them. When their eyes met the beautiful Light✠ of the angelic figures, they beheld their own faces looking back at themselves, as if they had been transported to another world of beingness. And The Woman conceived. 5

Afterwards, an Angel✠ appeared to The Man declaring that he must leave Peru with The Woman and take her to the north where The Child of Light✠ would come forth. 6

12 · HOLY ONES
GUARD THE CHILD OF LIGHT

AND THEIR PILGRIMAGE took them to Yucatan, Mexico. They settled in Merida, near the old ruined cities of the Mayas, and were accompanied by The Nurse, The Youth, The Nurse's younger son, her young daughter, and The Woman's first son. Together they lived quietly under the tropical sun, sustaining their bodies with natural raw fruits and vegetables, herbs, wild honey, and coconut juice. 1

At night, Holy Figures✠ stood around the mother's bed, guarding over the expected Child✠. Oriental figures they were, tall and cloaked in white and purple, and all those who were vigilant of the sleeping mother witnessed them. And in the fifth month The Woman fell ill, and the doctor advised that the unborn Child✠ be removed; for a tumorous condition prevented a natural birth and endangered the life of the mother. And The Man deliberated, taking The Woman to the island of Cozumel for peace and quiet.   2

One day, while swimming in the sea, The Man caught a glint of a lustrous white pearl lying in an open shell on the bottom of the sea. He attempted to reach it but could not, for a giant shark blocked his way. A ray from the sun penetrated the clear water and struck the gem, and the sea blazed like fire. And a Voice✠ came to him: "The pearl symbolizes the True Church. The Child✠ will restore and bless it. Seek to protect the treasure." The Voice✠ ceased, and the vision of the pearl disappeared while the strong currents carried him back to shore. 3

Shortly thereafter, The Man, The Woman, her son, and The Companions journeyed to America where The Man believed the cooler climate would save the mother and assure the birth of The Child.✠ 4

THE TEXT II

LIFE WITH THE CHILD

1959 - 62

13 · BIRTH OF THE CHILD OF LIGHT

THEY WERE GUIDED to New Smyrna, Florida, where they lived in a home on a hillet of thickets next to the sea, and the cool breezes of the ocean and sunlight did strengthen The Woman. 1

One night a brilliant ball of white light appeared from the east out of the sea and burned above The Man on the beach. And he made a sign over his breast with his right hand and looked towards the circle with a prayer on his lips, pondering its meaning. 2

And on the morning of March 16, 1959, under the sign of the fish, The Woman was with pain. At daybreak, eight months following conception, The Child✠ came forth like the rising of the sun, strong and perfect, and many came to gaze upon The Child's✠ beauty. 3

Great was the joy when mother and Child✠ returned home. And The Man baptized the baby, naming him Jamil,✠ which means "beautiful." But the joy was short lived, for The Woman grew ill with fever. And The Man remembered the words of The Angel✠ who said that she would bear no other children from the moment of The Child's✠ birth. And he feared for her life. The fever raged, and her hair fell out. A Great Light✠ burned about The Woman as if the Powers of Heaven✠ were consuming her very body, and The Man gave of his healing energy and prayed to God✠ to grant her life. The fever subsided, and The Woman's life was spared. And The Man rejoiced, for he loved her dearly. 4

But, as all things in the material world have a price, the laying on of hands to save The Woman had taken all his generated strength, and the healing power left him. 5

14 · OPPRESSION

FROM THE DAY OF HIS BIRTH, a Light✠ did shine about The Child.✠ At night he slept softly, almost as if in another world, and The Light✠ glowed about his person. He walked at an early age and often stood on the white sandy beaches on slight-built legs, his hair glowing like sun rays, waiting for sea turtles that often came on shore to greet him. And the sun browned him when he played on the beach from sunrise to sunset. 1

And in the springtime, flowers placed at his crib were in no need of water; for his Light✠ gave them life. And sparrows and hawks of the air came down to pay him tribute, for he was one with all life. 2

His food was simple. During his first months his nourishment was milk from his mother's breast, then small amounts of oatmeal, wild honey, fruits, nuts, and dainty green peas. 3

One day The Man observed The Child✠ looking at the sun. His eyes were two radiating stars, growing brighter as he raised a finger to his lips to throw a kiss to the sun and turn the Light✠ of his beautiful eyes on his father. And The Man knew that The Child✠ was of divine nature. 4

Inspired by The Child,✠ The Man did teach those who would hear, but he was oppressed by civil institutions. And The Man feared for the welfare of The Child.✠ A Voice✠ came to his Eternal Consciousness✠ forewarning: "Persecution comes if you remain. Return to your adopted land and raise The Child✠ in secret until the appointed hour. Be of good cheer for The Light✠ is with you." And before the year was over, they left America to dwell in Mexico where The Child✠ blossomed under the sun, and the mother regained her health. There, The Man celebrated the thirty-third year of his life. 5

Many followers visited The Community✠ to honor The Child✠ and study the teachings of The Man. And the infant Jamil✠ did smile favorably upon the yogi Seeress from America, and she did see his golden halo. And the Seer from Ireland looked upon him also and was inspired by his presence. A year later the family returned to Peru, sojourning in the city of The Woman's birth. 6

Each day The Man spent hours in the desert, oftentimes with The Child,✠ reflecting to the sun. They would return to the city radiant with energy, their persons glowing with Light.✠ And large crowds would gather around The Man and the wondrous Child✠, following in their footsteps as they walked the streets and plazas. And The Man grew concerned with all the attention, deciding to keep The Child✠ in the garden, away from the public, and directed his wife accordingly. But The Woman was filled with pride and delighted in the attention paid her son by the populace. 7

One day she took The Child✠ with her to the public market where an unusually large throng of curious adults and children assembled about The Child.✠ They pressed around him, touching his hair and pulling at his clothing, and Jamil✠ stood calm, though he suffered from the beams in their eyes. And they did take his energy by touching him. And The Man, hearing of the commotion, hastened to the market where he scolded his wife for displaying their son in public. 8

And a day came when The Man's spirit drew away from his being, and he retired to his bed too weak to walk. Once before he had experienced the desire to forsake the mortal world when The Angel✠ had come to him. This time he did not fight the feeling. His family and The Companions came to his bedside to say their farewells, for he was certain he would not see the rising of the sun. 9

That night, as he was contemplating the events that had led to his state, while the fragrance of the burning incense and the lights of the candles placed around his bed pervaded the chamber, his mind became still and his body weighty. He saw the smiling face of The Child✠ and his sun-like eyes radiating love to him. The Man realized he was giving in to some Dark Power seeking to prevent The Child✠ from fulfilling his mission on earth. And he resisted the temptation to leave the world before his allotted time. 10

In the days and weeks that followed, the curiosity of the people turned to contempt; for they knew The Child✠ and his parents were different from themselves. 11

They looked at the sun and were not blinded. 12

They did not eat animal flesh. 13

They spoke of a coming Christ Age✠. 14

Was not the mother of The Child✠ a divorced woman, bitter of heart? Was not the father a stranger from a faraway land? They were both sinners and heretics. And the magistrate did call them, testing their faith and asking if they believed in God✠. Again, they were oppressed. 15

15 · YUNGAY

ONE DAY WHILE PLAYING, The Woman's eldest son pushed Jamil✠ to the ground and, wanting to take advantage of his larger size, sought to hold the younger boy so he could not rise. But Jamil,✠ though younger by six years, was unusually strong; he stood on his feet, holding his brother at bay with one hand. And when the older boy attempted to struggle against the infant, The Child✠ pushed him gently, but firmly, across the garden, as if he were a leaf in the wind.1

A hunchback, who became one of The Companions of The Man, often visited the house. Life✠ had endowed him with a brilliant mind, and, being from a family of strong, tall, handsome brothers—scholars and professors all—he had from early youth sought the spiritual meaning of life. He came to be known as the Hunchback of God✠, for he was a metaphysician. And The Child✠ grew fond of the wise man. They conversed on philosophical matters, and the Hunchback of God✠ was amazed, for The Child,✠ but two and a half years old, already knew the deeper truths of creation. 2

During one of his visits, The Child✠ asked him if he liked music. Being a musician himself, the older man answered The Child✠ that he did; whereupon, Jamil✠ sat down and began to play on a piano. The Hunchback of God✠ was enthralled, for never had he heard compositions so like what one would imagine the music of the heavenly spheres to be. And no one could account for The Child's✠ knowledge of music or his mastery over the keys. 3

Shortly following this episode, a change came over The Child.✠ He often remained in the garden where he was found talking to unseen figures. He drew symbols in the sand with his fingers and spoke in a language that no one understood. And, in a dream, a Voice✠ came to The Man, telling him to take The Child✠ to the Andes for the time of the revelation was at hand. And he did take The Child✠ and his mother to the uplands, six months after arriving in the community of Trujillo. They were followed by The Youth, The Nurse, and the other Companions. 4

They settled in Yungay, an isolated hamlet of white-washed houses and red tile roofs, graced with royal palms and eucalyptus trees, situated in a valley of Peru called the Callejon de Huaylas. Bathed in whites and blues in the morning and roses and purples in the afternoon, the quiet village lay in the shadow of the towering snow-capped Huascaran. 5

And the natives accepted them with open arms, providing them with a spacious home and large garden in the center of town, and a forested hill of eucalyptus trees some distance from the city, facing the pinnacles of the Andes. The people rejoiced with the newcomers; the old Indian masons, descendants of the mighty Chavin, went to work clearing the Garden and laying stone pathways. Groves of eucalyptus trees were planted, and the natives cared for the land as if it were their own. 6

In the mornings, when the village sparkled under the sun's rays reflected on the snow, Indians dressed in red and brown ponchos came to the entrance of the house and, as silent as stones, sat outside the gate observing The Child✠ in the Garden. And The Child✠ looked at them with kindness for they were his brothers and sisters. He would approach and, laying a tender hand on their shoulders, speak to them in a voice that sounded like a morning bird saluting the sun. No one knew what was said, save the speaker and the listener. Once an old lady came begging for food, and The Man heard The Child✠ call her "akchii," which is the Quechua Indian word for "light."   7

And when the children of the village came to peer through the gate, The Child✠ gave his clothes and some of his toys to them; for they were poor, and it gladdened him to see them scamper away with laughter in their hearts. 8

And the villagers spoke of the marvelous Child✠ who had come to live in their midst. The elders looked away at the distant heights saying: "This Child✠ is like the summer that melts the snow and warms our hearts. Surely God✠ has sent us a comforter." And they called The Child✠ "El Niño." And the tale was spread here and there throughout the Andes. The Indians talked about him in the settlements and in the fields.   9

In the days and weeks that followed, father and son walked in the meadows and woodlands and often visited the great Temples of the Sun left by the ancient Chavin people who had been masters of the Andes three thousand years before. The Child✠ gazed upon the broken stones and the great granite columns, and he listened to the sound of the wind rustling through the branches of the tall eucalyptus trees that stood like giant sentinels. And he reflected upon The Sun,✠ communing in a tongue that only the spirit speaks. 10

Shepherds and peasants left their flocks and oxen unattended to walk in the footsteps of The Child.✠ Sparrows and hawks fluttered above. Grazing sheep ran beside him. And the fallen statues seemed to open their eyes, as if the light from his shadow, reflected on their mute faces, awakened them from along sleep. 11

Once The Child✠ came to the edge of a swamp crossed by a stream, and the multitude with him stopped. But The Child✠ proceeded swiftly over it, leaving faint impressions upon the surface. Eagerly, they awaited his return. 12

Returning home in the gathering twilight, the father carried The Child✠ in his arms, contemplating the events of the day. That night, The Man observed about the cradle a luminous glow made by radiant figures standing around the sleeping Child✠. They were robed like the Apostles✠, and one appeared to be Jesus✠ administering to the sinless infant. 13

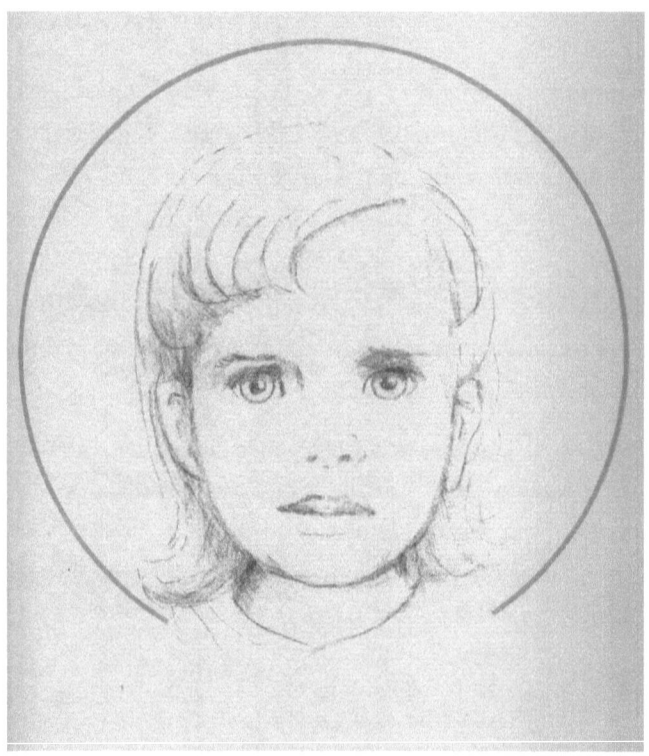

16 · BEATIFICATION

IN THE MONTHS THAT FOLLOWED, Jamil✠ grew even more beautiful. His eyes sparkled like diamonds set in a pure blue sky. From within his breast a Light✠ like that of a newborn star, illuminating a world of darkness and shadows, lit up his countenance. He was marvelous to behold. There was a radiance about him that turned his hair gold and his skin to pearl-like luster. And when he spoke, it was like a singing star sending its song throughout the universe. 1

One morning, at first light, The Man rose from his bed and found The Child✠ looking intently at him, lost in thought. It was a benevolent look, but The Man saw that Jamil✠ was seeing through him while communing with another world. He walked over to the crib and took the small figure in his arms. A soft breeze blew across The Child's✠ face, and the father remembered the prophecy that his son would never grow to manhood. He trembled at the thought and held the finely-built boy to his breast; he felt the tiny heartbeat that seemed to keep tune with the great universal heart of Heaven✠. 2

Sensing his father's pain, The Child✠ touched his lips with his delicate fingertips, then kissed his cheek. And The Man knew then that he was both a father and a disciple to the Seer-Child✠. 3

As the sun burned through the heavy layer of clouds, a cock crowed in the distance. The Child✠ laughed, for he loved all living things that saluted the sun. 4

And, as he often did when The Child✠ inspired him, The Man withdrew and wrote down the word-messages that came to him from the Light✠ of The Child's✠ eyes. 5

17 · HOMAGE FROM A WANDERER

LATER THAT DAY, a blind beggar visited the house, dressed in a poncho and felt hat. He was aged and wrinkled like the rind of a cantaloupe, and he carried a staff with two white feathers tied to the top. There was a great dignity about him. None had seen him before, but it was said by the folk of the uplands that he was an ascetic who had left his abode near the snowy peaks to visit The Child.✠ 1

For a long time he played on a reed flute, filling the air with haunting tunes, until one of the house servants went out with food for his bowl. As if called by the melodious pipes, The Child✠ went outside and led him by the hand through the gate into the Garden. He helped him sit down on a stool under the spreading branches of a tree, out of the warm rays of the sun. The two sat face to face. 2

And The Man, having heard the strange music, came into the green sanctuary and found the two together. So as not to disturb them, he remained behind a bush and listened to what was said: "Thank you, O Child✠ of the Universe, for admitting me into your presence." The beggar's voice was soft like wind blowing through a willow tree at twilight. "Little Child✠, for a moment I thought I saw light when you touched me. Can it be that my poor blind eyes can see only saints?" The Child✠ made no reply but gazed intently upon the older personage. 3

The old man spoke again, saying: "O Son of the Whole World✠, surely what they say is true: that you bless the land and its people. When you look upon me, I hear whispered words of the Sages of bygone days. Yet you speak not. Is it that an Angel✠ from Heaven✠ talks to the ear of my soul through the Light✠ of one so near the cradle? O Niño, though my descent is from the kings of old who once ruled the land, I am nothing more than a poor wanderer with nothing to give, save my homage." With these words he bowed to The Child.✠ And The Child✠ placed a tender hand upon the man's head. 4

Rising, the wanderer faced the house servants who had gathered at the edge of the Garden and said: "The old songs tell of a fair-complexioned boy who will regenerate the world. And the sign of his coming shall be a Great Circle of Light✠ in the sky. And the boy shall be our elder brother come to restore what was taken from us centuries ago. And the Tree of Life✠ that fed the First Man ✠ shall bear its fruit again. When this day comes all mankind shall be freed from the burden of Supay, the devil, and made to cease from ruinous wars." Then he turned to leave, saluting The Child✠ with his upraised staff. The gardener led him out through the gate. 5

18 · TRANSFIGURATION

ON A SUNDAY IN OCTOBER, Jamil✠ and his father were alone in the Garden. The Man was bent over an ancient manuscript, deep in study. The Child✠—the image of the morning sun still bright in his eyes—walked the paths deep in contemplation. And The Man observed his son communing with an unseen force, noting a stillness in the air. He put his book aside, clearing his mind so as not to disturb the Spiritual Communion✠ of the infant. 1

The Child✠ walked unshod, his little sandals, along with his cape, placed on the table under the fruit tree. Respectfully, The Man removed his own shoes, resting his feet on the warm grass. The branches of the stately eucalyptus trees were filled with birds, yet their voices were hushed. They, too, sensed this was not a day like other days; they waited expectantly, for there was something about The Child✠ that commanded attention. Every part of him radiated compassion. A faint smile traced his lips. His tiny hands were held behind his back. His head bowed towards the earth, he appeared to be directing his energies inwardly, to the center of his being. 2

For some forty days, The Child✠ had abstained from food. No force could make him eat, save some raw, green peas and a few grains of rice. He seemed to draw some form of nourishment from the earth itself, from the sky, the sun, and the few handfuls of water that he allowed to pass over his lips. Yet, something more sustained him. 3

The Child✠ was slowly withdrawing from the material world into another dimension of existence. Nevertheless, his was not the state of the ascetic who meditates within himself, leaving his body lifeless and unable to speak. Indeed, The Child's✠ form and being were very much alive and full of vitality. 4

And so The Child✠ strolled peacefully along, neither sad nor joyful, seemingly caught up in a heavenly reverie of his own making. Every part of him mirrored a veiled understanding of tolerance and love. He was at oneness with all the living things of the universe; at peace with God✠. 5

At one point, the father approached him, but The Child✠ placed his finger to his lips as if to silence him. He gave the impression of a bearded prophet, the recipient of supernatural knowledge. After some time, The Child✠ lifted his eyes from his downward glance and looked into the sun; fused with the center of the universe, his whole being underwent an alteration. 6

A golden halo surrounded his head, and Jamil's✠ body shone like a flame. As matter became spirit, The Child✠ was radiant beyond description. And all the living things and the birds in the trees rejoiced, singing a hymn to The Child;✠ for they wished to participate in his Living Communion ✠. 7

And The Child✠ turned and spoke to his earthly guardian, calling him by a new name. And The Man locked the name away in his heart, keeping it to himself. And the disciple looked into the shining eyes of The Child,✠ awestruck by what he saw; for rays of Light✠ flashed from The Child's✠ eyes, and they glowed a thousand times brighter than the sun. The mortal man was held spellbound, breathless, suspended in a world where space and time merge, and he was conscious only of the immobility of his own body. 8

As he stared into The Child's✠ eyes, The Man became aware of an angelic form materializing out of The Child's✠ countenance. To his amazement, he saw the face of the pure-spirited Angel✠ that had appeared to him six years before—the same that had risen him from the dead now personified in the form of a child. Light✠ upon Light.✠ He was being made to see that Jamil✠ had both a human and a divine nature. The Child✠ was revealing that it was he who had first called The Man out of the world to serve Christ✠. And The Man believed in the Angels✠ as taught in the Holy Books✠ and spoken of by Holy Men✠ of former ages. 9

Truly there were things beyond man's understanding. Whatever pride and arrogance, whatever trust in his own powers The Man had up to that time left him; for he knew that the small Child✠ before him was in truth the incarnation of a Being of Light.✠ 10

And the sun oscillated in the air, saluting the transubstantiated Being below. 11

Gradually The Man regained control of his senses and the eyes of The Child✠ dimmed, and the aureole around him was not as brilliant as before. 12

For the rest of the day, Jamil✠ allowed no one to come near his person. And when his mother returned✠, she beckoned to him, but he did not move. And when she approached, he held up his finger, saying: "No toca," which is to say, do not touch me. And The Woman was bewildered, and she clasped her son to her breast for she loved him. But The Child✠ cried out, turning his eyes to his father. Again The Man was in the grip of the two beams of light. And he saw the pain in his son's eyes; whereupon, he took him in his arms and carried him into the eucalyptus grove. 13

Thenceforth, he addressed The Child✠ with the respect a disciple would give a prophet, knowing that Jamil✠ had been anointed by God✠ for some holy purpose. 14

19 · THE LIVING COMMUNION EXEMPLIFIED

WEEKS PASSED like the rising and setting of the sun, and the holiday season drew near. The Child✠ loved to walk in the Andean pastures where he would move through the grasslands and thickets fleet of foot like a tiny deer. Often he was taken to the large eucalyptus grove on the hill provided by the natives, and oftentimes he would leave his father behind. And The Man was fearful that an animal might carry off his son. 1

Once a fox looked upon the infant, lifted its paw and followed his graceful movements with its sharp eyes, but allowed The Child✠ to pass unmolested. Another time, a grazing bull grunted at the little boy as he walked past its horned head, and again Jamil✠ passed unharmed. And a mountain lion peered curiously at the boy, gazing lovingly at him as if he were one of her cubs. And when The Child✠ entered a large cave in the heights above the village, scorpions scampered away, and when he touched them, they did not sting his tender flesh. And once, when he had reached a green valley beside a blue lake that lay under the reflected light of the snowy peaks, a king condor swept down from out of the sky, landing on a rocky pinnacle, and lifted its wings to the Blessed Child✠ as if saluting the sun. 2

Neither animal nor crawling thing, not biting insect nor stinging thorn, nor poisonous plant ever harmed The Child,✠ for all living things were his brothers and sisters. Indeed, The Child✠ always returned to his father clean and unmarked, little butterflies clinging to his shoulder or perched on a raised finger. Since he was attuned to the very heart of nature, she bestowed upon Jamil✠ her bountiful gifts, though by this time he did not eat any living thing—neither animal nor plant, nor the fruits thereof. 3

He communed with Heaven✠, partaking only of a holy repast that nourished the spiritual part of him and that in some secret way gave life to the physical. He lived on the heavenly Bread and the Cup of God✠, relating to all of nature, aware that the spirit lived in everything. 4

And Jamil✠ stood before the shepherds on the Andean plateaus, inspiring them by his presence. 5

All the while, The Man wrote down the Teachings and Sayings of The Child,✠ though much remained unspoken, for there were no words that he could speak to reveal the inner truth of his soul. But The Man listened to The Word✠ made manifest. 6

20 · THE FINAL MEAL

IN THE COURSE OF TIME, Christmas Day approached. And a delegation of villagers bearing gifts of flowers came to the house of The Man. And one of them stepped forward and spoke: "We would bring more, but we are poor. The stomachs of our children are empty, and there is little milk for the infants. Our youths leave before attaining manhood to seek work in the heartless cities of the coast, never to return. Our young daughters are taken from us to labor in the houses of the rich where they live among strangers. Our womenfolk are without hope and the men chagrined, for they are unemployed. We are pitiful people who struggle from day to day for existence. Many are the widows, the orphans, and the homeless. This is a poor Christmas for Yungayinos, for we have little to give one another. God✠ grant that you have come to help us in our hour of need." 1

And The Man came before them saying: "The Spirit of Christ✠ teaches that each man help his neighbor according to his means." And he employed several of the menfolk and gave away the accumulated wealth of the household for the benefit of the village. And when they had rejoiced, he invited them to a banquet, and they did partake with thanksgiving. 2

On Christmas night, The Child Jamil✠ sat at the table with those who had gathered around him. And there were eight. The table was laden with fruits and nuts, cakes and candies, corn, rice and potatoes, bread, and sweet wine. And The Man was asked to say grace over the food, and he hesitated, saying: "Think now, my beloved companions, of the thing you ask. 3

"Does not the whole world participate in an unending cannibalism, each thing living off another—slaughtering animal, fish or fowl, grain, and vine? Know that the wheat and the vine, the cane and the tree, and the fruits thereof were sacrificed for this meal. Did they not have a right to live? Do not the sacrificed have a place before God✠? While God✠ is present in all living things, indeed in all creation, God✠ is separate from it and transcends it. Who, then, sustains the eater? Whom should we thank for nourishment?" Then, he broke bread and raised a cup of wine, adding: "We are taught that this bread and this wine can be changed into the body and blood of the New and Eternal Covenant✠ which is Christ✠. We are also taught that, except we eat of the flesh of man and drink his blood, we have not life in ourselves." And they were all silent, everyone, and perplexed; for they had all been taught to say grace and partake of Holy Communion✠. 4

And The Man, speaking for The Child,✠ sought to explain his words, and he said: "We are taught that all things are cleansed with the shedding of Jesus'✠ blood and that through this blood we receive eternal redemption from sin. That when the bread and wine are consecrated and taken unto ourselves, we achieve a spiritual union with God✠. Is such union attained by the stomach? Bread and wine nourish the physical body, which is heir to death. Is not the corporeal body food for worms—the eater becoming the eaten?" 5

The Man walked over to the mystical Child✠ sitting quietly at the table and said: "We have seen how this Illustrious One✠ eats practically nothing, save a little water. He lives off The Light,✠ taking no life by which to nourish his body. Is he not nearer to God✠ than any of us? Is there not a celestial bread, a celestial wine for which we should thank God✠? We speak here of a nourishment that sustains the spirit. Man is made in the image of God✠ and endowed with spirit. The corruptible body is subject to the power of death because it lives only by taking other life. The spirit is incorruptible and immortal only because it is nourished by God✠. 6

"The reign of God✠ will come and the goodness of His Righteousness will be available to all men everywhere. And man's spiritual nature will live by a divine nourishment from Heaven✠, a hidden Manna✠ that extends immortal life. Through this Food, man will experience a new birth and cast off the old ways that place him in the service of material things. On this day man will heed the Will of God✠, called Christ, incarnate in man." 7

And The Man further said: "I have witnessed the consumption of this food by one among us who serves as a model and lives a Teaching so that we might follow. This Holy Food✠ is not given in any temple, but is everywhere, available to all in God's✠ creation. It is this Food that will turn men and women from idols of stone or silver set up in houses of worship. And they will experience God✠ by means of a higher spiritual faculty, knowing that the moral and intellectual strife of man's mind and corporeal body cannot fulfill his spiritual longing." After he had said these things, The Man did eat of the bread and did drink of the wine, and said: "I do this in memory of a Holy One✠ who taught and lived among us in ancient times, and who acknowledged a greater gift from God✠ which shall be extended to mankind." 8

Thereupon, The Child Jamil✠ took up a fragment of bread and ate of it. And he drank some water from a cup. And after he had done this, a Light✠ shone about him. And The Man did see four Holy Figures✠—luminous Angels of God✠—standing around The Child.✠ And this was the last common meal of which The Child✠ would partake, though none at the table knew of it, save his father and the Beings✠ who guarded and attended him. 9

21 · THE MOUNTAIN FALLS

FIESTA TIME DREW NEAR. Men and women left their fields and their orchards and entered the village to participate in the celebrations commemorating the birth of the Infant Jesus✠, for they were Christians. Great was the joy of the people. For three days there was dancing, eating, and drinking. They formed colorful processions which wound through narrow streets towards the church. There, they placed baskets of flowers, picked from the mountain sides, at the feet of a wooden statue of Jesus✠, asking the idol to smile favorably upon them. 1

The market places were filled with happy peasants. The weavers, the potters, and the dye makers sold their wares, as did the fruit vendors and all the merchants gathered to peddle their goods. And the dancers and the singers came, and everyone clapped. Sky rockets burst above, and a procession went to the Church of the Lord of Miracles✠ in nearby Ranrahirca where candles were lit. Merriment was everywhere. 2

And on the third and final day of the festivity, the populace awoke at dawn with gratitude for another day of merrymaking. And they sang praises to the Lord✠. And the flute players and the drummers played for them. No one thought of the morrow. It was the 10th of January, 1962. 3

Twilight approached. The sun sank below the horizon and the last rays of light glimmered on the summits of the towering Huascaran, turning its snowy face a vivid purple. The multitude continued their festivities, dancing and singing with joy. None heard the muffled sound of the ice and snow that cracked and fell from the mountain. And the earth shook, and the spirits of the dead seemed to awaken in their tombs to shout to the living, but no one gave heed to their calls. 4

The Man, who had been writing, perceived the hush of nature as the birds grew silent. And when the sound of the falling mountain struck his ears, he lifted his eyes to the heights and saw a cloud of snow billow up against the streaking rays of light. And he was disturbed; for he sensed danger, and The Child✠ was not with him. At that moment, The Woman, who had been away in the city of Huaras, returned with Jamil✠ who came into the Garden to his father's side. 5

Whereupon, a great avalanche of rock, ice, snow, and mud swept over the nearby villages of Ranrahirca, Yanama Chico, Schacsha, and Uchucoto, carrying with it thousands of the living into the river and thence to the sea. 6

As light gave way to darkness, terror stricken survivors who had sought safety on the summits filtered into the com- munity to tell of the dreadful occurrence. When the landslide struck, the sun was darkened and the moon shed no light. The earth trembled in anger, and many feared the mighty Huascaran would fall again. It was a terrifying night. And at daybreak, though no eye saw the sun rise from behind the mountains, they awoke from their slumber. And a great multitude congregated and walked to the edge of the flow—with stunned faces, they gazed upon the desolation. 7

The once happy community of Ranrahirca and its inhabit- ants lay beneath the earth. All was gone, save the mud and the rock and the ice. And the village elders wondered what they should do. Many swore at the mountain, shaking their fists in the direction of the citadel covered by clouds and mist. Others buried their heads in their chests and walked away knowing that the life they had known was gone forever. Not a few of the younger men accused God✠ of having no mercy, and they turned away from the pitiless firmament, bitter of heart, for they felt the people had suffered enough over the centuries. 8

But the older ones still believed in God✠. The church was filled with worshipers. Still others turned to the old deities, sacrificing and burning incense in the ruined temples and shrines of their forefathers. Everywhere people fell to their knees before powers greater than themselves; and, by whatever name, called upon the gods to have compassion upon them. 9

Carrion-feeders came to feast upon the putrefying flesh of man and animal. And the plagues did come. And famine spread—many more died. Children, ill from polluted water, ran to their mothers, seeking comfort in the folds of their skirts. Nothing could stave the germs of sickness, though herbs and old remedies were administered. Women held the lifeless remains of their sons and daughters tightly to their heaving breasts, rocking them to and fro upon their knees, weeping and wailing, disbelieving that extensions of themselves were dead. And the menfolk stood helpless, looking heavenward with unseeing eyes, unable to understand the awe-filling forces that ruled their lives, powerless to do anything but suffer the indignities of losing their offspring. 10

And the townsfolk came to the house of The Man, for they feared the loss of all the children. Knowing of their suffering, he pledged to journey to the capital and seek aid, for the world did not yet know the magnitude of the tragedy that had befallen the isolated hamlet. He would ask for a purification system; for the people, in their ignorance, did not realize the water was poisoned. 11

Thereupon, The Man did prepare to travel, forced to leave The Child Jamil✠ in company with The Nurse, The Companions, and the house servants. The Woman would accompany him—she believed she could help him bring back assistance to the community. And they did leave, promising to return soon. 12

22 · THE COMFORTER

MANY QUIT THE BODY, releasing their spirits into the care of heaven. Others remained at the altars and temples, day and night. for they feared another catastrophe. And The Child Jamil✠ was a comfort to the villagers. He stood out like a beacon of light walking among the diseased and dying, speaking to them of things unknown. And the people saw that he was with them, and their hearts were strengthened. And they said: "This Child✠ is the Light✠ of the world," for they believed. And The Child✠ said that sacrifices and invocations could not save the spirit. And both the living and the dead drew upon his Light✠ and energy, surrounding him like a forest. And he sustained them. 1

And The Man and The Woman returned after a lapse of ten days. Wearied and sick of heart, they walked through the desolate streets towards the house. And they saw the suffering souls looking at them with hollow eyes and drawn faces. The poisoned water still flowed from the fountain—the purification system had been denied—and the living drank it out of need. Like a thick fog, a pall of wretchedness hung over the community. 2

And when The Man and his wife entered the Garden, they found the entire household ill and prostrate—The Youth, The Nurse, and the other Companions. All lay helpless on the ground, victims of the pestilence. And in a corner of the Garden, they observed The Child✠ sitting beneath the spreading tree, mindful and self-possessed. His small frame was pale and drawn—the same as those unfortunates they had seen in the village—which told them the body of Jamil✠ was diseased. Yet a Light✠ shone about his person, and his eyes were those of an aged personage who had lived a thousand Christ✠ lives, now transformed into a Divine Child✠ awaiting the final mergence of his being with God✠. 3

And again The Man remembered the prophecy that his son would vanish to another world after three years following his conception. And the thought caused him pain. 4

23 · THE PROPHECY

APPROACHING THE PURE CHILD✠, The Man bent down to take the boy into his arms. And Jamil✠ extended his glorified hand to touch his father. And he wiped away his tears with a kiss. Then he stood up and looked deep into the older man's eyes; and The Light✠ flashed again. And he spoke to the inner ear of The Man's Eternal Soul✠, saying: "Weep not, father, for I shall not pass until the allotted time. If you would mourn, mourn for those poor, suffering souls here. For I say unto you that the mountain shall fall again in the space of time, long after the memory of what has occurred here has faded from their minds. Nothing shall remain of this city, save the covered remains of the dead and their habitations. 1

"And men in the four quarters of the world shall weep for these souls, unaware that the dead will be witness to that which is destined for the whole world. And you shall see in time to come that this shall be the beginning of sorrows spoken of by former Prophets✠ inspired by God✠ the Father. The human family has turned from God✠ and trusted in worldly ways, spurred on by the physical sciences that deny that man is the bearer of the human spirit. Some would have the children of God✠ believe that man has no purpose, that his identity and selfhood is destroyed with the loss of the physical body. Such philosophy has caused the negation of human feeling, and nature shall respond in like manner. 2

"The Prophets✠ have always striven to teach man how to live in harmony with nature, and their teachings were for the purpose of meeting human needs for the day and age. Four times the earth has been depopulated through floods and catastrophe caused by nature in rebellion. I say unto you that the children of tomorrow will not inherit life on this planet if it occurs again. It is in the name of future generations that we come to teach. 3

"And you shall warn the living here of what is to pass. But they will heed not your words. They will mock you and scoff at you, all of them, even those of your own household, and turn once more to the old ways, believing all things will continue as before, taking the name of the Prophets✠ to their own blind ends. And the earth shall tremble. 4

"Let all the people of all nations learn from the events that will come to pass, here and in other places in the valleys and heights of the Andes, that the whole race of man can be swept away by fire from the sun and the stars. As Noah taught and warned his people, you shall do unto the world." And when Jamil✠ had thus spoken through the Eternal Light✠ of his Being, the older man, speaking with his tongue, answered: "But what shall be gained if you pass from the world? Would not more be achieved if you remained here with us, teaching and instructing us in the way to salvation?" 5

And a second time The Child's✠ eyes transmitted The Light,✠ and The Man heard the words as before: "I am the Universal One✠, spoken of by Teachers✠ of old; I have appeared at sundry times and places in man's evolution; I am he who the Prophets✠ have said would come again at the Final Age of the world. I come as a child and leave as a child, so that no man may lay hold of me, abuse or punish me as they have done to so many of my beloved Brothers✠. It is not fitting that men bend the Prophets✠ to their own selfish and ignoble ends. 6

"God✠ will call out of the nations of the world a chosen people who will sustain a New Sun✠ and generate a new race to inherit a new earth that will grow out of the old. It will be a planet of Light,✠ like The Sun,✠ brilliant and fiery, under the direct rulership of God✠. Man will save himself by generating a new Body of Light✠ within the manifesting Christ✠ that is given for the salvation of the human family, under a system to be taught by an Order of wise and holy men and women. This Order shall be under God's✠ supervision and guidance from a World on high, and I shall not pass from this world until I have named and appointed the first of the New Prophets✠ and instructed him in the New Tenets.✠ He will be the recipient of a supernatural knowledge and oversee The Order of which I speak. 7

"The aged religions founded by my Brothers of Light✠ and beloved of man mustneeds be dissolved; for they guide men in archaic moral and intellectual disciplines which of themselves are not sufficient for a new spiritual birth, nor do their sacrifices and prayers teach the human race how to elevate themselves under the New Sun✠. 8

And a second time The Man appealed to Jamil✠ not to pass from the world. And The Child✠ spoke to him in Light✠ for the third time, saying: "You mourn the passing of my material body, O father of my flesh. Know you not that I go to a place where life never ends?" And The Man wept, moved by emotion. 9

And for the fourth time the Light of The Child's✠ eyes spoke: "Death cannot claim my person or the Spiritual Body✠ which I have manifested before you—this same Body which all men have inherited from God✠ the Father, but has wilted and all but died because the nourishment thereof has been denied it. But I say unto you that God✠ has extended the Fountain of Light,✠ the Holy Fire✠, again, and man's Spiritual Life✠ shall be reborn like a living flame burst into light at this great cycle of spiritual regeneration. My brief sojourn upon the planet has been for the sole purpose of revealing that message from God✠ the Father, and to exemplify what is possible for all men who walk the earth. It is not proper that I linger. What can come of it? Those too weak to find God✠ within would worship me and put words in my mouth, thereby building a religion that would hold mankind in further ignorance. Nay, let no man use me. I say unto you that no man shall touch the body of a Holy One✠ again. I come to fulfill the religions of the Ancient Ones✠, our beloved Brothers of Light,✠ and our authority mustneeds be from the safety and sanctuary of Heaven✠. 10

"Some will compare me to my beloved Brothers of Light,✠ grown noble over the centuries, saying I was only a small child to whom you have built a memorial. And they will scorn you, saying that the age of the Prophets✠ is over, that God✠ and Christ✠ are no longer manifest. Such are men of little faith who belittle God✠. And you shall know them by the emptiness in their souls. They do not understand the Religion✠ of the Holy Ones✠, which is truly dead to them. 11

"While my Teachings may appear to take away the religion of my beloved Brothers of Light,✠ I say unto you that their original Teachings are lost to the world, polluted as the water which courses through my vitals and causes my body pain. It is good that this New Teaching✠ come into the world to unify the human family; for I say unto you that Christ✠ is alive throughout the whole universe as the fitting culmination of all Prophets.✠ 12

"Today there is much disunity. Each one goes his or her own way, thinking that each has an answer to personal salvation. Such cannot be, for all things in the universe follow certain immutable laws. Procreation and generation of the physical body are good examples of this. Men following these laws flourish; otherwise, they perish. Spiritual birth is the same." 13

And The Child's✠ eyes appeared flaming like a sun, and he was beautiful beyond words. 14

24 · THE DIVINE COMMAND

AND THE MAN GAZED at The Light,✠ hearing the final words spoken to his Eternal Soul✠ from the abode of Heaven✠. "Nothing shall be as it was; the old passes away. A New Sun✠ and a new earth created for a just end is the gift of God✠. And the message of God✠ has come to heal all men. The old religions and the Prophets✠ shall live afresh in the manifesting Light.✠ Go forth. Teach the message to responsible men and women of the planet, revealing the source of a new knowledge from God✠ the Father. They shall learn new ways, living a higher social, moral, and spiritual Order under God✠. And a great good will come of it. But take heed of the manifesting Darkness and the Evil One who shall seek to lead mankind astray. You will hear him speak of unnatural things, and his followers will be known by their desire for spiritual anarchy on earth which will lead to the extermination of the greater part of the race. And many will take the name of Christ✠ in this effort. But I say unto you that a new people casting off the old ways will elect to hear the Word of God✠. And they shall be known by their Light.✠ 1

And The Man addressed Jamil✠ asking: "How shall all these things be accomplished?" And the radiant Child✠ answered: "You shall be given, through inspiration from God✠, a New and Higher Gospel✠, and you shall write down that portion to be revealed publicly, retaining the greater portion thereof in secret to be administered to those who would dedicate themselves; for it is not good to distribute the whole Teachings, lest they be abused by arrogant men. Begin first with the Christians, restoring what has been lost to them, by decoding the writings of the New Testament and revealing The Religion✠ that supplements that which was previously given. You shall found a New Order✠, ordaining Teachers to a New Ministry who shall be the successors of The Church and the New Apostolates✠. And Christ✠ shall manifest through them." 2

And The Man asked The Child Jamil:✠ "Are you the returning Jesus✠? Or Elijah✠?" And Jamil✠ answered: "There are many who believe that the Holy Ones ✠ recorded in their own Scriptures and Holy Books✠ are unique, that there were no other Christs✠ before or after them. I say unto you that I am unlike mortal men. Have you not seen Holy Prophets—Jesus ✠ and Elijah✠ and many others—attending my person? We are all Brothers of Light✠, immortal, holders of the Office of Christ✠. A New Christ Age✠ is upon the universe, manifesting for the salvation of all living things. Teach this." 3

"By what authority shall I do these things?" asked the disciple. "Surely they will think me mad." And again The Child's✠ eyes blazed like flame, penetrating The Man, and he spoke in The Light✠: "Your authority shall come from the living Christ✠, the same that brought the Christian religion into being first among the Jews, and later among the Gentiles. The times of the Gentiles are fulfilled. The long-promised Coming✠ for which Christians have waited since the passing of Jesus✠, who is manifest in The Sun✠ as surely as if he were walking the earth, is upon the world. But no mortal may call upon the name of Jesus✠ as a personal savior as before. The same Christ✠ that moved him, my beloved Brother, the same that moves all the Immortals,✠ is manifesting in every living thing through the Sun of Righteousness.✠ It is the responsibility of every Christian who calls upon Jesus✠, or God✠, to reflect the Christ Force✠ for the overall good of the universe. 4

"I say unto you that the Last Age is upon the earth. This you shall preach to the Christians. And you shall say that your authority comes from God✠ the Father. Who among the living shall contest such authority? Surely no Christian who believes in the hereafter. After preaching to the Christians, take the message to all of the human family saying to them that that which was promised by the founders and the Prophets✠ of their respective religions, my beloved Brothers of Light,✠ has come to pass. 5

"A universal way of unity, which men of all religions may live, has been extended. It is valid for all men of all faiths, be they Moslem, Buddhist, Hindu, Taoist, Confucian, Zoroastrian, Jew, Christian, or a member of some other belief. It is authoritative and fused with the manifesting Christ Force✠; and the truths of this Teaching will be known to the developed spiritual senses, for spiritual truths do not register upon the rational mind or the physical senses. God✠ speaks to mankind through Christ✠ and the Sun of Righteousness✠, but all men do not know how to listen. You shall teach them how to hear God's✠ Word for themselves in the new spiritual birth which comes by the divine grace of God✠ for the redemption of His children who are part of the Godhead✠, but lost in the world of the senses." 6

And after he had said these things, The Child Jamil✠ closed his eyes, for he was weary. And The Man took him in his arms and carried him to his bed, which was placed on the upper level with its head to the north between two rows of eucalyptus trees; and he rested. 7

After doing this, he joined The Woman, and together they attended The Youth, The Nurse, and The Companions, preparing medicines, hot water, and herbs. 8

25 · THE CHILD RETURNS TO THE WORLDS OF LIGHT

FOR MANY DAYS, the Blessed Child✠ remained in his bed, reflecting within himself and refusing to eat. And his personage shone bright like gold. But, freeing himself from the pain of his body, the pure infant took leave of his bed; gathering his strength, he visited each member of the household: The Nurse, The Youth, and the rest of The Companions, touching them with his glorified hands. And they did recover from their infirmities. 1

And Jamil✠ spoke to The Youth as an aged patriarch, in sympathy and understanding, for he saw that The Youth was inflamed with a desire to know the truth. He had been the earthly companion of The Child✠ since his birth, and Jamil✠ loved him. And the infant looked into the young man's eyes with Light✠ that penetrated his heart. And he told him that it is not by individual effort alone that one advances towards understanding of God✠, but by obedience, discipline, and service in fellowship; it is one thing to possess knowledge, another to experience it. And of what value is it to know if one does not know God✠? Those at the beginning of the path must not stray, thinking that mind can find wisdom; only the spirit understands wisdom. And The Youth understood his words without comprehending their full meaning, for his life's pursuit still lay ahead of him. 2

And Jamil✠ laid himself down again, calm and peaceful, communing with an unseen force. And those gathered about wept; for the thought of the successor to Christ✠ and the Prophets✠ of former times leaving this world caused them suffering. All were humbled by his loving kindness and the bliss they felt in his presence. And The Man did visit The Child✠ once more, exhorting him to remain. And Jamil✠ arose and stood on weak legs looking at his earthly father and disciple. Then he put the index finger of his right hand to his lips and smiled, shaking his head. And his father was silent. 3

And Jamil's✠ eyes did speak again to the spirit of The Man, saying: "I am the last of the Holy Ones ✠ to visit the earth. Watch. You shall see a new form arise out of the remains of my mortal body—and it shall be a Body of Light✠. This spiritual resurrection is a promise to all men and women of the earth that they are sons and daughters of God✠ the Father. In spirit they are immortal. And you shall teach all the peoples and nations of the earth of what I have exemplified here. Man is in the last and final age. It is for him alone to seek and find God✠ in the manifesting Light of Christ✠ given through the Sun of Righteousness✠. 4

"Following my entrance into the Worlds of Light✠, my beloved father and brother in Light✠, let no member of the Order cherish my material remains. Keep no lock of hair, no nail clipping, no piece of my clothing as a relic. Remember me in spirit, and the life that God✠ gives to all the family of man by virtue of the redeeming force manifesting in the sun and the stars. And humanity shall be freed from earthly saviors and man-made religions governed by self-appointed priests who would misguide humanity. After my passing you will take the Sacred Teachings✠ of Light✠, entrusting them into the hands of the Guardians of Light✠."5

And the kind Child of Light✠ kissed his earthly guardian on the cheek, thanking him for attending him during his brief sojourn on earth. And he took both his hands into his own, as had the Angel of Light✠ years before, and said in the Light✠ of his eyes: "I anoint and ordain you to the New Apostolic Ministry in the name of God✠ the Father, and the

Universal Christ✠, and in the name of all the Holy Ones✠ of old who are alive and with me now. And you shall ordain others into the Order teaching man's pre-eminence and responsibility to the fellowship. And if any man or woman ordained in any Church taking the name of God✠ the Father, or Christ✠, oppose this Teaching, let them know, they who call themselves Christians are denying themselves. And the prayers and supplications generated by their intellectual faculties, though they live moral lives, shall be empty words in space; for God✠ hears only those words spoken by the spirit of man. Let no member of the Order condemn these unfortunates, but pray for them that they might hear The Word✠. For it profits not God✠ if the world is further polluted with unkind thoughts toward my beloved Brothers and Sisters in Light✠. Too many have taken the name of God✠ the Father and Christ✠ unto themselves for selfish and gainful reasons, bringing sorrow upon themselves in the end. Be tolerant and long suffering, teaching by example, not by force or threat of words. Of what value is the teaching if it profits not man for whom it is intended?" 6

The Man did see The Light✠ manifesting about the blessed Child✠ as a thousand shining eyes, and Jamil✠ lay down on the couch with his head to the north. And The Man placed in his tiny hands, held open and upraised toward the sun, a Bible and a golden cross with chain. And Jamil✠ gently pushed them aside, saying in the Light✠ of his eyes: "The Word✠ is not contained in this book, nor in this cross of gold." And the disciple was bewildered. 7

Seeing this, the Master Jamil✠ spoke once more saying: "Think not that I am being disrespectful; The Word✠ lives in the Spirit of Christ✠. The Cross✠ lives in God's✠ New Sun✠. We have come to release the Christians and the peoples of other religions from bondage to words they do not understand. Too long have our brethren been led astray by those who preach from the Books, not understanding the message. For I say unto you that God✠ summons man to live the Holy Word✠. We will give a supplement and open the Book of Life✠, and all the peoples and nations of the world shall understand the hidden meaning of Scripture now given to mankind in the last and final age. And God's✠ New Sun✠ shall scorch the earth with the Heavenly Fire. And it shall be a balm to the Children of Light✠. And the Dark One shall no longer deceive the world, for all men shall know the truth by the birth of the Cross of Enlightenment✠." 8

After these words, Jamil✠ spoke the last and final time to his father, saying: "Now go from here, for your love of me keeps me from my Work✠." Whereupon, Jamil✠ called his mother to comfort her. 9

And he looked into her eyes and saw not The Light✠. She was his earthly mother, and his love for her was beyond human understanding—a kind that generates the sun and the stars. He lay looking at her with great compassion, knowing that his refusal of the food she offered caused her pain. She loved his being and could not understand his message from the Most High✠: All life is spiritual and that in spite of the death of his body, he would find Life✠ everlasting. Yet, as every mortal, she must learn her way, and that those in the service of God✠ must endure worldly hardships. 10

And they bathed The Child✠, dressing him in clothing of white and blue. Afterwards, The Man journeyed to the coast, as instructed, leaving his son in the care of his mother. 11

That night, at the last watch, Jamil✠ breathed for the last and final time, his open eyes facing the star-studded sky. And when his mother visited his bedside at midnight, she found him lying still, and she gave out a shout of anguish. Alas! the Divine Child✠ had passed out of earthly existence, consumed by the fire of his own Light✠. 12

And those who were witness to the event said that the earth shuddered as it had when the mountain fell, and the stars shone more brightly than before. And some experienced a heavenly music seen as starlight but heard by the inner ear. 13

And The Man felt The Child✠ freeing his spirit from the prison of matter. And he wept, knowing that his son had left him. It was midnight, January 29-30. Four months had elapsed since The Child's✠ arrival in the Andes. 14

26 · AT THE SEPULCHER

THE MAN LEFT the lands of the coast, returning to the heights of the Andes. And when he had come to the house, he found The Woman, The Companions, and the house servants gathered in the Garden, crying and lamenting. He embraced them all, holding back his own tears. Then, he went to the upper room where the remains of the blessed Child✠ lay at rest amongst a bed of fragrant blossoms. 1

For a long time he stood looking at the beautiful face still in death. Lifeless eyes stared back speaking no words of Light✠. The boy's pale lips were unmoving; and when The Man took a gentle hand into his own, he felt as if his heart would burst with pain, for he knew that never again would he feel the warm touch of his son. When again he looked upon the colorless face, he saw his own face there, then, the reflected faces of the whole human race: men, women, children of every color—white, black, red, yellow, brown. Yet they were all the face of Jamil,✠ who bore the soft lines of an aged patriarch. 2

The Man remained in the upper room the rest of the day, recalling the events that had transpired since The Child✠ had come into the world. When light faded and night came down upon the Andes, he returned to the Garden, now filled with beautiful bouquets of wild flowers plucked from the hillsides by a multitude of Indians come down to honor the memory of The Child✠. And the flute players, lamenting the passing of the golden-haired infant and all the other children of the heights and valleys, filled the air with selected refrains. And the drummers beat sullenly day and night as if signaling the gods of ascending spirits. 3

With the coming of dawn on the second day, Jamil's✠ remains were prepared for burial. And his father, in company with The Nurse, anointed the twelve openings of his immaculate body—his hands, feet, and forehead—with oils and placed salt on his tongue with a precious stone of jade. And while they were doing this, those gathered in the Garden below noted the peace and calm in the upper room. An aroma of azahares, roses, and gardenias perfumed the ether. And when the remains of the Lustrous One✠ were brought down, a radiant Light✠ shone about his figure, golden like the sun, and they believed his soul had returned. And they likened him unto a saint, for none had seen such beauty before. Lovingly, they wrapped him in cloth and covered his yellow ringlets of hair with a headpiece, placing his remains in a wooden casket lined with soft material of perfect white. And they placed therein offerings of perfume, incense, and flowers. Having done these things they covered the box with glass, for they could not bring themselves to hide his loving face that reflected the benevolent rays of the sun. 4

At high noon, the mourners set off on foot towards the high hill overlooking the city, followed by a delegation of villagers. There they would entomb the earthly remains of Jamil✠ in an unmarked tomb prepared by stone masons. The Man had selected the hill, so often frequented by Jamil✠ in life, where the eucalyptus grew. Arriving at the foot of the hill, the procession stopped. The villagers treated them with consideration and left The Man, The Woman, The Youth, The Nurse, the rest of The Companions, and a single stone mason to continue on, for they respected their grief. And the eight of them went forth through the eucalyptus grove, ascending the height. 5

The Man and The Youth, who bore the casket, fell to their knees three times, and their strength did ebb. During life, Jamil✠ had been light as the wind; in death, his fragile remains had become heavy as stone. And they were mystified. 6

They reached the burial ground at the summit, and sat down to rest at the base of a great rock hewn by the stone masons to form a receptacle for The Child.✠ Few precincts of the world could equal the natural beauty of the hill which, from earliest times, had been a holy shrine to the people. Situated in a time-honored spot, known as the spacious land between the four rivers, with the towering snow-capped Andes visible to the north and the spreading fertile valleys lying to the south, the pinnacle caught the first rays of the rising sun as it came up over a green height to the east, and it remained illuminated while the sun inclined toward the west disappearing behind the purple heights of the Cordilleras. And when the moon arched through the sky, it could be seen clearly day or night from one end of the horizon to the other. No king could claim a more venerable resting place for his earthly remains. 7

When they had gathered their strength, they lifted the wooden casket up to the rock-hewn sepulcher and placed it in the crypt, elevating his head and pointing it to the north, and inclining his feet to the south, so that he faced the sky in an upright position. And they interred his earthly possessions with his remains, looking upon his face for the last time with love and tenderness. And The Man, dressed in a suit of white linen, spoke with heavy heart: "Friends, brothers and sisters, we place this Holy Child✠, whose spirit has departed his earthly remains, at rest in this rock. During his lifetime, but three short years from the time of his conception, we have been honored to live in the shadow of his Light✠. Now that he has gone from our midst, we shall miss that Light✠

for we all loved everything he did and said. Above all, we loved him for what he was. We do not understand why God✠ chose to speak through a small child for so short a time, but in those 1260 days we saw Christ✠ exemplified here on earth. We saw how the earth devoured his outer being, how he suffered and died in a world of sorrow. Remember how the living looked upon him, filling their emptiness with the beauty of his form and spirit, yet he passed out of this world without complaint—calm, resolute, and resigned. We saw him transfigured and beatified. We saw how the spirits of Holy Ones ✠ communed with him, how the living Angels of Light✠ spoke and administered unto him. We know from this he was more than a babe—his inner being was immortal Light✠. How many of us gathered here on this rugged height, in the crags of the Andes, ever expect to see another such as this Child✠?" 8

And The Man, speaking with an awakened spirit, placed his hand on the sepulcher and continued: "This Child✠ was a Teacher of divine concepts who assumed painful but necessary human form as an instrument of God✠. Following his mission, he has abandoned this world. From him we have learned the meaning of Christ✠—that the office of Christ✠ is assumed by many. Surely Christ✠ has returned to the world as was promised by the Prophets.✠ Some will say that Jesus✠ or Buddha✠ or Elijah✠ or Viracocha✠ or Zoroaster✠ returned in the form of a child. But we now know and understand how God✠, having no form or substance, clothes Himself in terrestrial garments, thus becoming visible to man; yet, God✠ is one and undivided. 9

"From the events that have transpired, we know that the Spirit of God✠ manifests in different forms—as Christ-like Beings✠ who live among us for a short time and direct us to the Godhead✠. Christs✠ are all one, undivided. It is only their human nature that separates them in certain times and places. These things we have learned. We have gathered here to return the remains of the outer form of The Child✠ to the earth. The inner personage has returned to the Worlds of Light✠ whence he came, forever freed from the power of death. Yes, the spirit will live on. This you must all believe. Now let us close the sepulcher." And each in attendance did place a stone therein with his or her own hands, and the stone mason laid flat stones over the opening, cementing them together. 10

At three o'clock in the afternoon they closed the tomb. An undisturbed quiet enveloped the height. In the course of time, they heard a great fluttering as if of wings, and, looking upwards, they saw a great multitude of eagles and condors silhouetted against the heavens tracing a large circle above the tomb. And their numbers darkened the sky. Rare birds of all assortments banded together, filling the branches of the eucalyptus trees, some chattering exuberantly, others singing blithely. An unseasonable swarm of gilded butterflies clustered about the sepulcher, turning it a golden color, and they were left unharmed by the birds. And a glowing hummingbird flitted about the crypt. And they saw a great dove across the face of the sun. 11

And at that moment water flowed out of the side of the sepulcher. And all assembled on that majestic height witnessed these events. 12

And when these things had occurred, a great wind arose, sending dark clouds scurrying past the face of the sun. And The Man and his Companions clung to the earth and the rocks, for the wind was strong. And it thundered, and the rain fell. And they lifted their eyes heavenward, observing the darkened sky and the serpentine forms of the clouds swallowing up the sun like a flying dragon and shutting out the light.

After this, the sun came out and the wind subsided. Then, The Man, the six Companions, and the stone mason made their way down the hillside for home. 13

When the sun set, it turned fiery red and it oscillated from side to side. And The Man could not look at it. But he heard a voice telling him to return to the sepulcher on the fourth day following the passing of The Child✠ and await a sign.   14

27 · THE SUN OF RIGHTEOUSNESS PROCLAIMED

WHEN NIGHT WAS COME, the earth rocked to and fro as if seeking to unite itself with The Light✠. And the stars fell from Heaven✠ in a great shower. And an Angel✠ appeared to The Man in his dreams saying that he should await the signal of God✠, The Cross by which the world was enlightened, at the tomb of The Child✠ two days hence. 1

With the coming of dawn, the members of the household arose with the sun. And when they entered the Garden, they found three rose bushes in bloom; they counted two roses of white, five red, thirteen yellow, and twelve pink. And they were amazed that all the shrubs had flowered from one day to the next in the whole village. 2

All spent the day and the night in prayer, fasting and mindful of the events predicted by The Angel.✠ And when the second day of February dawned, the sun burned bright in the heavens. And they did return to the tomb, and there awaited the promised event. And at noon, when the tomb cast no shadow, behold! a great halo formed around the sun. They stood breathlessly looking in wonder and awe. Then a circle of rainbow colors, like crystal spheres, blue at the center and red at the outer edges, encircled the sun. In the heart of the radiant globe, a white Cross✠ appeared. And they feared the Last Day was upon them. And they trembled, forgetting the promise of the Angelic Host✠ and the message of The Child.✠ For an hour the heavenly blaze burned in the firmament. And The Man looked upon the sun, and the image of Jamil✠ appeared across the sun, radiant beyond words—his countenance bright and his hair white as snow. And The Child✠ was holding The Sun✠ in his arms, over his heart. And The Man saw a gate to another world. Again he saw the four Guardian Angels✠ around The Child✠, and on the right hand side of The Child✠ he saw the image of Jesus✠ and the Apostles✠ witnessing his appearance. And he heard the voice of Jamil✠ as music, speaking to the Light✠ of his Eternal Soul✠, saying: "I am resurrected." And the disciple knew that The Child✠ was redeemed from the earth. 3

Again The Voice✠ spoke, and it was like the sounding of a loud trumpet: "The Hebrew Prophets,✠ through whom God✠ spoke, wrote: 'Behold, the day cometh that shall burn as a furnace, and all the proud and wicked will be like stubble. And the day that cometh shall burn them up, saith the Lord of Hosts✠, that it shall leave them neither root nor branch. But unto you that fear my name shall the Sun of Righteousness✠ arise with healing in its rays, and you shall go forth leaping as calves to pasture. And you shall tread down the wicked, for they shall be as ashes under the soles of your feet in the day that I am preparing, saith the Lord of Hosts✠.' 4

"And did not Jesus✠, my beloved Brother of Light,✠ answer, as recorded in the Books, when questioned about this future event?: 'The coming of the Son of Man✠ will be like lightning coming from the east and flashing in the west. Wherever the corpse is, there shall the vultures gather. Immediately, but after the tribulation of these days, the sun will be darkened, the moon will not give its light, and the stars shall fall from the sky, and the Powers of Heaven✠ shall be shaken. And then the signs of the Son of Man✠ will appear in Heaven✠, and all the peoples of the earth will beat their breasts, and they will see the Son of Man✠ coming in the clouds of Heaven✠ with great power and glory. And He shall send Angels✠ with the sound of a loud trumpet to gather His chosen from the four winds, from one end of Heaven✠ to the other.'" 5

And the risen Child✠ said: "The incarnation of God✠ the Father is come to the world through the Sun of Righteousness✠, healing and sustaining the human family and restoring the Life of Righteousness✠. As the seed of man enters the womb of woman and life cometh forth, so shall a heavenly Seed✠ enter the spirits of men and women, and a new birth shall occur. And the life thereof shall be of God✠. And death shall not claim this new Body of Light✠ and the Spiritual Consciousness✠ therein. And the Christ✠ transmitted in the Sun of Righteousness, and indirectly in all living things, down to the smallest atom and particle, shall incarnate within the soul of mankind. And every man and every woman shall know that they are one with the Godhead✠, divine and immortal. 6

"As the senses of the material body have perceptual experiences, as the mind reasons or thinks, remembers or wills, the Spiritual Body✠ shall perceive, and man's Spiritual Consciousness✠ shall understand and commune with God✠. Know that it was experienced by ordained Teachers who came to instruct men in the will of God✠; yea, by Jesus✠ and the Prophets✠ of your own religion as well as by those Teachers of other world religions. The Incarnation of Christ✠, as a Universal Spiritual Force, is not the property of any one religion or of any one man or woman. Christ✠ is the Consciousness of God✠ the Father, who gives life to His spiritual beings, as your parents gave you life; for you were not self-generated, which proud men forget in their selfish lives, losing sight of their spiritual origins. Know you that the spiritual senses are as different from the material senses as man is from God✠ who gave him life. No person can commune with God✠ by means of the physical senses.

It is for this reason that mankind has misunderstood the Prophets,✠ for man is unable to comprehend God✠ having fallen away from the Life of Righteousness✠. 7

"These Prophets of Righteousness✠ came to teach man a Righteous Spiritual Life✠, as God✠ intended the life of man to be. They were raised up by Christ✠, who quickened their spirit and gave life as does a parent. By these means, they were able to communicate with God✠ and interpret His Sayings to man's Christ-Consciousness✠. There are among men and women of your Christian faith those who believe that by worshiping Jesus✠ or by adhering to rituals, dogma, or other matters of faith and belief, they will be saved. This is in error. It is not by faith or belief that man is redeemed from death. If the spiritual faculties be not developed, or given life, man fails to share the divine life. I say unto you, how can there be life if man and woman do not propagate? They think, by reason of their rational mind, that spiritual life is an occurrence comparable to the theories of their scientists who say that life is a thing of chance, an accident or trick of fate. Has any man observed an unlawful universe where there is life? Is not all governed by some law or guiding force? Know that the spiritual universe is lawful, governed, and guided. Know that spiritual life is given by a new birth and consciousness. 8

"Priests and ministers of your faith claim to be the direct successors of Jesus✠ and the Apostles✠. They believe their teachings, based on the Holy Books✠, to be the Word of God✠. But I say unto you that the Christian message was lost to the world soon after the judicial murder of Jesus✠ and his immediate disciples. The clergy would have the laity believe that the shedding of Jesus'✠ blood was for the redemption of man and a necessary sacrifice to God✠. Around this teaching was built a religion which conceals the true message. I speak to you in words you can understand, for you are of Christian tradition. Know, then, that the

Church of the old dispensation fulfilled the earlier Hebrew tradition. Since the beginning of time, God✠ the Father has revealed through His glorified Prophets✠ spiritual wisdom that would satisfy man's longing for unity with God✠. The Christian tradition, and the Hebrew tradition before it, nourished guardians of holy teachings now lost to the world. No book contains the true message. No scripture alone can support a religion without the living Prophets.✠ Look around you. Where are they today? 9

"A New Community✠ shall come into being as a fulfillment to the Christian Church. It shall be truly universal, valid for any man or woman who longs to experience God✠ through a new, spiritual birth, regardless of his or her religious tradition. And a new race shall grow up, nourished by the Light✠ of Christ✠ manifesting in the Sun of Righteousness✠. And this Community✠ shall go out into the world, at an appointed time, and instruct the Christians in the New Advent✠, revealing the Sacred Teachings which shall be entrusted into their care for dissemination to that portion of mankind who shall receive them. The Seals✠ shall be opened and The Teachings revealed to all the religions of the world. And if any mortal or church leader challenge this authority, the Community✠ shall say unto them that a New Creation✠ is coming; yea, it begins now—a world of Truth✠ and Life✠. None can stay the rays of Christ✠ in the Sun of Righteousness✠. It is for each man and woman to choose whether they shall live in The Light.✠ God✠ seeks to immortalize the whole of the human family, but men reject new teachings; they ask for signs, for proof, for miracles, not realizing the spiritual birth afforded is the Miracle of Miracles✠. 10

"Be ever mindful that the destiny of the world depends upon righteous men and women, for they alone can sustain the Sun of Righteousness✠ and the Universal Christ✠ from going out and darkening the world at the moment of a New Creation✠. Teachers of former times failed in their efforts to sustain the Spiritual Sun✠ of which I speak. Think not that the Prophets,✠ abused in person, and whose Teachings have been corrupted by wicked and selfish men, are content. They cry out to God✠ to assist them, and He has heard their appeals and sent into the world the unified energies of each and every one which forms the Universal Christ✠. 11

"Many will question that a babe could stand with the older Prophets✠ who attained manhood; yet, I am The Child of Righteousness✠, the Son of Man✠, prophesied by Holy Ones✠ to come unto the world in the last and final age. While the Light of God✠ did enter into my spirit and gave me Eternal Life✠, I was born of your seed as a testimony to the New Man✠ destined to inherit the earth. It is good that men do not worship or adore me. My merits are truth, mercy, goodness, healing, and life everlasting, which I have exemplified. My elder Brothers of Light,✠ the Prophets✠—loved and known to all men—are the Overseers of this holy mission. Their Light✠ shines through the Sun of Righteousness✠ with Christ✠ manifest in the world, given through the grace of God✠ the Father. 12

"It is proper that men know that the Divine Self✠ is immortal and co-existent with God✠ the Father. Instruction in this rebirth mustneeds be overseen by Teachers unified into a whole, living organism of Light✠ animated by Christ.✠ Go forth and build the Order, ordaining such that qualify in the teachings. Above all, unite the Order as you see this heavenly effort united on high. Go forth knowing that I go with you in company with the Heavenly Host✠. Let all men know that the Spirit of Christ✠ and the Sun of Righteousness✠—the Bread of Life✠—shine on all nations and peoples equally. In this way, they will understand our purpose. Seek not to convince men through argument or appeal to their rational minds; speak instead to the spirit; teach them the way through the Light.✠ Once you leave this place, return not. Refrain from exhuming the tomb to see if my material body has ascended, for I say unto you there is resurrection only in the spirit. Flesh and bones do not inherit the Kingdom of Heaven✠. 13

"For a season you will wander, and I will guide you to the sacred valleys and mountains beyond the snow-capped Andes; and you shall dwell in the forsaken temples built by forgotten peoples, some of your own race, and you will learn the fate of mankind led astray by the Powers of Darkness. There you will record the Books✠ and Doctrines✠ of this old-new Religion of Light✠ come to earth from on high. I will manifest to you in your dreams, and you shall see my face in the Sun✠. And the Powers of Darkness shall visit the earth again, seeking to harm the race and this teaching. Those you love and trust shall turn against you, stripping you of all your worldly goods, and you shall be sorely tested in mind and spirit, imprisoned and made ill of body. And you shall be abandoned and left to your tormentors. This shall be the period of your exile. In the end, you shall be raised up and restored to health. And you shall see that righteous living and trust in God✠ is the only true reality as taught by the Prophets.✠ And you shall migrate, after a space of ten years, leaving the land of your tormentors, strong in the knowledge that those called by God✠ must not isolate themselves from their own people. And you shall take the Books✠ and return to the land of your birth, teaching those pre-ordained to hear; you will urge the New Community✠—the chosen people of God✠—to build first in America, not in Jerusalem or Rome or any other place, the New Temple of the Living to bring forth Children of Light✠ for a New World. 14

"You are destined to be the First Teacher of Righteousness in the New Community,✠ and the sun will announce your return in a display of energy which will be the beginning of solar manifestation of a kind not known in the world before. And men of learning shall be troubled. And the Golden Age of The Sun✠ will have commenced. And the Chosen shall go forth exemplifying and teaching a New Life✠ in harmony with Christ✠; and all disease, which is the result of man working against the forces wherein he had his origin, shall be banished forever. And by so doing, he shall live to great ages as he did in ancient times when sages and Prophets✠ exemplified God✠ in their daily lives. Only those who eat the fruit of God✠ shall be sustained; those others shall continue as before; yea, shall perish in the end because they chose to live in ignorance of God✠ serving artificial and lesser gods. In this Great Age of Light,✠ every living thing shall be at peace with one another. Think not that the Reign of God✠ shall commence at once. Perfection requires patience and time in the world. There shall be great conflict between the Powers of Light✠ and the Powers of Darkness. Take care that those blessed ones who will follow the teachings be not led astray by Beings of Darkness fallen from Grace. This is the great spiritual war spoken of in former times. Already these forces are at work: the anti-Christs, who would abuse the sun and the energies thereof, and the God✠ mingled therein, to punish the Children of Light✠ as they have done in ancient times. Be on guard and teach against them, for they prevent man from returning to God.✠ 15

"From the beginning, God✠ caused the True Religion✠ to come into the world under different names. These religions sought to restore moral order in the world and lead mankind towards universal brotherhood. Today moral order, in the individual and among nations, has been replaced by selfishness and a fear that spreads around the world. Anarchy threatens on a level never before known. Terrestrial concepts have replaced celestial concepts. Priests of God✠ have been replaced by priests of the earth, men who would abuse the resources of the earth and the universe for vainglorious ends, by so doing, invade and impose themselves upon the Kingdom of God✠. The end result shall be revolution in society and a universe in rebellion, causing earthquakes, floods, famines, plagues, and wars. Human existence shall perish if the madness created by the Powers of Darkness, seeking to exterminate the race, does not end. And if man continues blindly ahead to his own destruction, then we shall make a place for the Community,✠ as provided to peoples in times past, and it shall survive the disorder. 16

"In this last and final age of the world, the Universal Religion✠, the true religion, has come one more time from the mouth of God✠ the Father manifest through the Living Christ✠ and the Sun of Righteousness✠. And the sign is the Cross of Enlightenment✠ which shall be seen by all peoples by means of their spiritual sight. Man may be regenerated because of this Religion✠, turning from destructive ways and regaining The Way✠ to salvation. Many religious and civil leaders, believing that things will continue as before, shall try to impose themselves in the Era of Christ ✠ by clinging to the old and attempting to tear down the new. Know that they have no authority over this Religion✠. Those who would speak against the Apostles✠ or Ministers of this Religion✠ cannot darken God's Light✠ which is irresistible and more powerful than worldly powers. It comes to alleviate the ills of the world and is, therefore, truly universal. All Prophets✠ of all ages—the Holy Spiritual Order of Elders✠—who have risen in the Light✠ shall manifest in The Sun✠ with Christ✠. They do this to restore man, their younger brother, who has lost his way. 17

"The words that I speak, or may speak, are limited by your own understanding. Therefore, let the Word of God✠ speak to your Spiritual Consciousness✠ so that you may understand. And let all humankind listen to the Word. Fear no evil save the Darkness of which I speak. The Angels of Light✠ and the Son of Man✠ shall protect the human family." And The Man felt the Breath of God✠ upon him, and he heard the words: "As I anointed and ordained you in the flesh during my earthly sojourn, know that I anoint and ordain you in Spirit✠ First Apostle of the Community.✠ Go forth ordaining others under new authority granted by God✠ the Father. Remember that Light✠ gives Life✠: Death comes from Darkness." Then the Vision of The Child✠ faded in the clouds. But the Cross of Enlightenment✠ shone over the face of The Sun,✠ burning radiant for another hour. And everyone in those Andes was witness to it. 18

And on the fourth day of February, the sun and six planets conjoined in Aquarius. And The Man saw great signs in the heavens. And the anti-Christ was manifesting. Whereupon, his body and mind and soul suffered turmoil. And the struggle continued through the sixth day, it being the eighth day following the passing of The Child Christ✠. But The Man prayed to God✠, looking upon the New Sun✠ and asking The Light✠ to assist him. The Child Christ✠ heard him and sent an Angel✠ to comfort him in his dreams. And the Darkness lost its powers over him. 19

Thereafter, The Man began the Great Work✠ east of the Andes. 20

www.ingramcontent.com/pod-product-compliance
Lightning Source LLC
Chambersburg PA
CBHW030157100526
44592CB00009B/330